POWERFUL PROJECT LEADERSHIP

Wayne Strider

MANAGEMENTCONCEPTS
Vienna, VA

MANAGEMENTCONCEPTS
8230 Leesburg Pike, Suite 800
Vienna, VA 22182
(703) 790-9595
Fax: (703) 790-1371
www.managementconcepts.com

Printed in the United States of America

Library of Congress Cataloging-in-Publication Data

Strider, Wayne, 1947–
Powerful project leadership/Wayne Strider.
p. cm.
Includes bibliographical references and index.
ISBN 1-56726-147-7 (pbk.)
1. Project management. I. title.

HD69.75 .S775 2002
658.4'04—dc21

2002019877

ABOUT THE AUTHOR

Wayne Strider's career spans 27 years, including 17 years with the former McDonnell Douglas Corporation and 10 years with Strider & Cline, Inc., which he cofounded. Strider & Cline is a management consulting firm offering project planning reviews, project implementation reviews, project retrospectives, and organizational assessments to information technology organizations.

Known for his ability to demystify the intersection between human and project management issues, Wayne helps executives, project managers, and technical professionals deal effectively with the inevitable human issues that can jeopardize the success of IT projects.

TABLE OF CONTENTS

FOREWORD

Have you ever worked on a project that ran into serious snags? Or a project that was canceled after significant time and expense? Or one that delivered an acceptable result, yet the people involved would rather have jumped off a cliff than work together again?

How many of these situations were caused, at least partly, by people problems?

Invariably, the quality of work on a project depends on the quality of the experience among those engaged in the project. Yet most of what's been written on how to achieve project success focuses on the technology of projects—the tools, techniques, processes, methodologies, standards, procedures, protocols, and checklists. These technical tools are critical in managing projects; if you don't apply sound management practices, project failure is inevitable. But when things go awry among the people engaged in a project—when stresses emerge . . . or tempers flare . . . or uncertainties arise . . . or self-doubts fester . . . or people behave like, well, people—sole reliance on technical tools is likely to exacerbate rather than resolve the problems.

What's needed in these difficult circumstances is powerful project leadership—leadership that focuses on working with people so that everyone can do their best project work. Indeed, if you exercise powerful project leadership, you will be far less likely to experience difficult circumstances in the first place.

But learning how to use your power appropriately in leading others—and really "getting it" in a deep-down and lasting way—doesn't lend itself to simple checklists or the team-building exercise du jour. It's difficult work—work that Wayne Strider has spent many years studying, practicing, and helping others understand. His considerable experience has resulted in a book that can benefit anyone whose work involves interacting with others.

Powerful Project Leadership will challenge you to consider your own behavior and to deepen your understanding of what helps you work effectively and what gets in your way. It will also help you understand why others behave as they do—and how to have them understand you better as well. In addition, you'll become more skilled at recognizing the signs that something is wrong on your project. You'll gain insight into those stomach-churning times when your project makes you want to run away and hide. You'll better appreciate how to have more time when you're sure you have too little.

This book will help you acquire a new toolkit for project success, and you will find yourself drawing from it frequently.

Employees, and entire organizations, are gradually becoming more receptive to considering the human component and its undeniable impact on project outcomes. Until recently, it was anathema in the workplace to even hint at the existence of emotions. Employees were expected to leave their feelings at home; after all, there was work to do! Yet, it's our very attempt to suppress our humanity that contributes to so many project problems in the first place.

Fortunately, we're now seeing a gradual change. At project management conferences, the sessions that focus on people skills are drawing large crowds. Consultants like Wayne and his wife and partner, Eileen, are increasingly being invited into organizations to help management take an honest look at what's going wrong in their projects and how they and their employees can work together to achieve their project goals more effectively. People have become more than merely curious about how to handle this "people stuff" better; they seem hungry for guidance in how to do it.

Wayne deeply understands these human issues and is a master at providing this guidance. Best of all, he is skilled at communicating it in a practical manner and with a caring, down-to-earth tone.

This book became a resource for me even as it was being written. I hope you find it as valuable as I have.

Naomi Karten
January 2002

PREFACE

For nearly three decades I have participated in, led, reviewed, and consulted to information technology projects. Project leadership is a difficult role. Project leaders are often measured and evaluated on the basis of their personal effectiveness at working in groups.

Eighteen years ago I was introduced to the Satir System through my association and eventual work with Jerry and Dani Weinberg, Jean McLendon, and Hugh Gratz. The Satir System is a system of therapeutic beliefs, models, and techniques for human communication, growth, and change created by Virginia Satir, an American family therapist. People who become proficient in her techniques are often able to perform difficult roles effectively in groups—such as leader, facilitator, or negotiator—even when those groups are experiencing chaotic situations. Adapting techniques from the Satir System has made me much more effective in my work with project teams—both leading them and consulting to them.

This book is my attempt to integrate and share what I know about projects with what I know about the Satir System. What I have learned is that project leaders can be more powerful when they respect the needs of those they lead without ignoring their own needs, and vice versa. I have also learned that projects are shaped by their contexts and contexts are in turn shaped by their projects. Project leaders can be more powerful when they understand and enter that dynamic, and thereby influence the shaping of their project's context.

This book is for people who want to become more personally effective at leading project work. These people might have job titles such as project manager or director, program office director, program director, project technical lead, project lead, principal architect, project architect, subcontract management manager, quality assurance director, or client relationship manager. People with all sorts of titles, none of which have the word "project" in them, find themselves leading projects of one kind or another. Some people, such as human resources professionals, may not lead projects but may work with people who do. This book is also for them.

There seems to be growing acceptance of, and even interest in, the dynamics of people doing technical work together. Many people know at some level that the quality of their experience working with other human beings affects both the process of producing the work product and the work product itself. They want to know what makes it hard for people to work together, how we often make it harder, and how we can make it simpler. They can find some of the answers in this book.

Difficulties that surface when working in groups or teams transcend tasks and technical activities. These difficulties involve interpersonal relationships and individuals' feelings. For that reason, anything that discusses these difficulties is often viewed as "soft" or "touchy feely." I interpret these terms as a comment about the degree of comfort one has dealing with what may be perceived as emotional or personal issues. Some believe that their role as leader requires that they avoid anything emotional, either in themselves or in anyone else. Some believe that expressions of anger or frustration are okay, but only in the context of exerting authority.

It is also important to realize that identifying and learning to effectively address the difficulties that arise when working in groups and teams is an utterly hard-headed and practical task. Although these difficulties may transcend the project tasks and activities, they often are the major inhibitors to getting the work of the project done. Those of you who may feel uncomfortable with some aspects of the approach taken in this book also know how uncomfortable it is working in an environment that suffers from seemingly intractable or chronic problems. To the skeptics, I suggest that you turn first to Part Three to see some of the practical, project-based approaches it offers and then go back to the beginning to get the foundations for initiating change.

I have worked with individuals who routinely share deep issues and emotions. They do not do this because it is comfortable. Even in a safe environment, it is hard work. They do it because they value the learning and sense of connection they get.

Many call these issues *people stuff*. I have been told that some people are starved for understanding of people stuff. This book is to feed those starving and also for my own learning. Part of my own learning process includes communicating to others what I've learned.

Many times in training situations, I have worked with willing individuals to help them untangle a messy interaction while an audience observed. Some observers have commented how moved they were. Often they express that they wish they could straighten out their communication with certain individuals back at the office. They want to know where they can learn to do what I did. This book is for them.

Keep in mind that the approaches offered here are not always easy. Like anything worth learning, it takes practice to develop expertise in applying these approaches and gaining the most benefit from them. I can testify that the effort is well worth it.

Wayne Strider
May 2002

ACKNOWLEDGMENTS

This book could not have been completed without the contributions of many people. I acknowledge the following people for their contributions to the improvement of this book through reviews, discussions, exercises, and examples.

Marie Benesh
Esther Derby
Carmen DiMichele
Jiro Fujita
Peter Hayward
Nyra Hill
Steve Jackson
Howard Karten
Nicholas Kirsch
Cathy Kreyche
Mike LeStrange
Michael Magnum
Jean McLendon
Bill Pardee
Sue Petersen
Sharon Marsh Roberts
David Schmaltz
Sheila Smith
Patricia Snipp
Robert Snipp
Myra Strauss
Eileen Strider

I also thank my client organizations as well as many participants of the Problem Solving Leadership workshop, the Congruent Leadership Change Shop, the Performance Development Program, the Personal Development Workshop, and the Leaders' Forum.

A special thank you to Cathy Kreyche, who asked me to write this book.

Many thanks to Naomi Karten for writing the Foreword.

A special thank you to Patricia Snipp, Robert Snipp, and Eileen Strider, who helped me create the first outline in a cabin at Nebraska's Mahoney State Park.

My gratitude to Eileen Strider for her encouragement, inspiration, patience, support, and love.

All people, projects, and client organizations in the stories and examples used in this book have been disguised to protect their identities.

INTRODUCTION

Most of us spend a lot of time in the presence of others both at work and in our personal relationships. As project leaders we depend on others to do the essential work of completing the project. Your time with others at work can be unproductive and frustrating when, for example:

- Your project is in trouble because you can't get the cooperation you need from other project managers.
- Your team stops working, claiming "We can't do our work because they won't give us the information we need."
- You know you should deal with a problem employee, but you avoid doing so.

How do you increase the productiveness of your time with others? That is what this book is about. First, though, it is necessary to develop common concepts and a language for talking about approaches to enhancing your power as a project leader.

The concepts of *self*, *other*, and *context*[1] underlie the structure of this book and mirror its three major parts:

- Part One: Leading Yourself
- Part Two: Leading Others
- Part Three: Shaping Your Project's Context.

---

[1]The concepts of self, other, and context as a model for congruence are based on the work of Virginia Satir. Virginia Satir, et al., *The Satir Model, Family Therapy and Beyond* (Palo Alto: Science and Behavior Books, Inc., 1991), p. 65.

In essence, the concepts of self, other, and context are the foundation for powerful project leadership. My premise—and my experience—are that project life, indeed life in general, is simpler, more productive, and more enjoyable when:

1. I am aware of and using my own power (*self*).
2. My contact with others is respectful and caring (*other*).
3. My responses seem appropriate given the current context (*context*).

These are the three components of what Virginia Satir called "congruence." They do not come easily. Being aware of and using your own power, making respectful and caring contact with others, and responding appropriately to the current context, all in the present moment, are probably the most difficult work you'll ever do. You won't do it perfectly the first time, or ever. But you can, with practice, achieve what my colleague Jean McLendon calls "moving from excellence toward perfection."

To understand how to lead yourself, lead others, and shape your project's context, you first need to understand the concepts of self, other, and context.

SELF

Many of us have been taught not to draw attention to ourselves. We learn lessons like "don't be selfish" and "put others first." We learn some of this in our religious training, our public education, and our families. Some of us learn these lessons too well, though, and do not assert ourselves even when we need to. "Self" in this book means *I am*. *I am* a being of worth, valuable beyond measure. *I am* a miracle of light and life. I don't have to earn my worth. I come into the world worthy. I have many resources within myself to help me grow, learn, and change, including my physical, intellectual, spiritual, and emotional parts.

My perception of myself—my "self"—is called self-esteem. My perception of myself may not always match my intrinsic worth—that is, I may not always feel like I am valuable beyond measure. When this happens, my worth hasn't changed, just my perception of my worth. I can modify my perception if and when I am able to let in new information about myself or put the information into a different context.

It's easy to take ourselves out of the picture when leading a project. When preoccupied with what the customer wants, what our boss wants, and what our teammates want, we can quickly forget our own wants and needs. Imagine leading a project when you are out of the picture. It simply doesn't work very well.

"I am aware of and using my own power."

When I say I'm aware of and using my own power, this means:

1. I feel valuable and I value others.
2. I am aware of my internal resources and limitations.
3. I am secure enough to express my own thoughts and feelings even when they could be unpopular.
4. I consider my own needs.
5. I take responsibility for my actions and responses, including mistakes.
6. I take risks, knowing that sometimes I will fail.

OTHER

"Other" in this book means any human being I interact with who is not me. We humans are all alike in some ways. For example, we all:

- Are born relatively small
- Have bellybuttons
- Are valuable beyond measure, according to most religious and philosophical beliefs.

We can also be very different from each other. We may have different physical characteristics, genders, religious beliefs, ethnicities, sexual orientations, educations, occupations, politics, psychological types, financial resources, or ways of leading projects. There are so many ways for us to be different from each other. One of Virginia Satir's therapeutic beliefs was that people connect on the basis of being similar and grow on the basis of being different.[2] With so many differences come lots of opportunities for growth.

From my perspective, when you and I interact, I am "self" and you are "other." In the same way, from your perspective, you are "self" and I am "other."

"My contact with others is respectful and caring."

[2]Handout, Satir's Therapeutic Beliefs, Satir System Training, December 3-8, 1999.

When I say my contact with others is respectful and caring, I mean:

1. I treat the other person as valuable.
2. I consider the other person's needs.
3. I am attentive and fully present with the person.
4. When I don't understand the other person's behavior, I try to give it the most favorable interpretation I can.
5. I speak for myself only.
6. I say "yes" and "no" with integrity, not defensively or aggressively.

SELF AND OTHER INTERACTING

When you and I interact, if either of us:

- Is not aware of and using our own power, or
- Is not respectful and caring of the other,

then our communication may be extremely difficult, with a high noise-to-signal ratio. The interaction is so loaded with useless or confusing information about the self or the other that the useful message or signal becomes buried and hard to find.

noise = useless or confusing information
signal = useful or helpful information

For example, say I am leading a project that has missed two critical deadlines. You are one of my technical leads. I am frustrated and angry. You have just told me that your next deliverable might be a little late. I say, "It's all your fault that this project is in trouble!" (shouting loudly and pointing my finger at you).

My contact with you is not respectful and caring. I load you down with my frustration and fail to address the project's difficulty in any meaningful way. Secretly, I don't feel valuable either. But I can't say I don't feel valuable even to myself. Instead, I project my feeling of low value somewhere else by blaming you. Blaming you is a way of protecting myself. When I blame you, I am not aware of, nor am I using, my own power. The noise in the interaction is high and the signal is low. The high level of noise—my blaming—prevents me from learning anything useful (signal) about what is wrong with the project. With my blaming approach, I'm unlikely to get you listening or to communicate in any helpful way to get the project back on track.

Continuing with this example, you say, "I guess you are right. I'm lousy at this work. I don't deserve to be on this project. I'm so sorry. Please forgive me." (Your head is low, avoiding eye contact with me, and your voice is soft and halting.)

Clearly, you do not look or sound like a person who feels valuable. You do not seem to be aware of, nor using, your own power. Again, the noise is high and the signal is low. You are making a comment about your (low) sense of power and competence and are obscuring the message about the difficulty on the project. Your placating response is neither respectful nor caring toward yourself. And you are unlikely to be able to help me address the real problems because you are too busy feeling worthless.

Let's see how the same interaction could be different when you and I are both aware of and using our own power, and our contact with each other is respectful and caring.

I say, "I'm worried about this project. We've missed two critical deadlines and I need some ideas on how we can make up the time. I trust your experience and I'd really appreciate your help with brainstorming some ideas. Would you be willing to do that?"

You say, "I'm relieved to hear you are worried. I'm worried myself. It's a bad sign when milestones start slipping, and I have some ideas that might help us get back on track. Sure, I'll help you brainstorm. Let's sync up our schedules."

The second interaction is more powerful because:

- Real human contact is made around an unexpressed but shared feeling—worry about deadlines being missed.
- Both you are I are taking responsibility for solving the problem.
- It is much more likely that the problem will be solved because we are both focused on the problem rather than on each other.

SELF AND OTHER IN AN ORGANIZATIONAL SETTING

"Self" and "other" can also apply to groups of individuals. Teams, groups, and organizations can get into the same kinds of difficult dynamics with each other as individuals can. The following table presents some possible combinations of "self" and "other" in an organizational setting. The multiple occurrence of "your software team" is not a mistake. Each occurrence is paired with a different "other" representing a group with which your software team might have to interact.

Self	Other
Your software team	Another software team
Your software team	The testing group
Your software team	The user management group
Your application development department	The customer support group
Your project team	The project office
Any team, group, or organization	Any other team, group, or organization, larger or smaller

For a team, group, or organization, "aware of and using my own power" might translate to:

- We matter. Our work is important to us and our company.
- We are creative, productive, and competent.
- We don't always agree among ourselves. You can trust that we each speak our truth.

- We do what we say we'll do. We make mistakes and we learn.
- We can't avoid risks so we try to manage them.

For a team, group, or organization, "my contact with others is respectful and caring" might translate to:

- We treat members of other groups as valuable. Their work is important to them and to the company.
- We are focused and give our full attention when we are with members of another group.
- When we don't understand another group's behavior, we try to give it the most favorable interpretation we can.
- Individuals in our group do not speak for each other. We do not speak for other groups.
- We take our commitments seriously, so we are careful with our yes's and no's.
- We willingly sacrifice individual needs when it's best for the group.

When teams, groups, and organizations work with each other in these ways, a similar kind of powerful result can happen because:

- Real human contact can be made.
- Such groups are more likely to share responsibility for solving problems.
- It is much more likely that problems will be solved because such groups are focused on the problem rather than on each other or individual personalities.

CONTEXT

"Context" in this book includes elements such as purpose, place, time, roles, conditions, and objects with which "self" and "other" operate. The elements of context also include air, temperature, smells, light, sound, and color. My colleague David Schmaltz calls context the "soup" that we're in.

Some of the soup is self-imposed—the agreements you make, the roles you accept, the opportunities you decline. Some of the soup can be other-imposed, such as the building you work in, who has the right to tell you what to do, or federal regulations with which you comply. Some of the soup is neither. It just is. It is the fabric of what we call "reality," like the number of hours in a day or weather conditions. We may be aware of all, part, or none of our soup.

"My responses seem appropriate given the current context."

When our responses seem appropriate to our context, we call that being *in context*. When our responses do not seem appropriate to our context, they can seem irrelevant, confusing, or meaningless to others. We call that being *out of context*.

Here are two examples of being *out of context*:

1. You are in a project meeting for the Zealous Zucchini project. You are to present your go/no-go criteria and status for that project's upcoming "go-live." Instead, you report on the restructuring of your organization.
2. Your colleague takes you to lunch at a vegan restaurant. Without looking at the menu, you ask the server for a hamburger medium rare.

The elements of context include:

- *Purpose*: The reason or end result toward which you are working. For example:
  —Make millions of dollars.
  —Analyze a problem.
  —Choose from among several alternatives.
  —Learn from one another.
  —Have fun.
  —Inform.
  —Provide a service.
- *Place*: The physical location and the characteristics of where you happen to be, such as:
  —Your office, building, city, state, country
  —Sound
  —Light
  —Color
  —Smells
  —Temperature
  —Air quality.
- *Time*: The present moment or some other reference made to time:
  —The present moment
  —A chronological history—yours, mine, an organization's, a problem's
  —Time zone differences
  —Standard or daylight savings time
  —Twelve-hour clock versus 24-hour clock
  —Measures of time such as years, months, days, hours, seconds, or nanoseconds.

- *Roles*: Your assigned functions and responsibilities:
  —Project leader
  —User
  —Sponsor
  —Database administrator
  —Developer
  —Software manager
  —President of the company.
- *Conditions*: Circumstances and events that may or may not be controllable and that affect your interactions with others:
  —Overrun project schedule and cost
  —Currently defending a lawsuit
  —Losing market share
  —Company about to go public
  —Labor strike
  —High turnover
  —Natural disasters (flood, earthquake, tornado, hurricane).
- *Objects*: Physical artifacts that define aspects of one's interaction with others:
  —Purchasing procedures
  —Contracts, agreements, expectations (explicit or implicit)
  —Project plans
  —Policies, procedures, or standards
  —Information systems
  —Development and production environments (developer workstations, servers, LAN, WAN, file structures, configuration management, etc.)
  —Physical plant (conference rooms, work stations, copiers, voice systems, lighting, ventilation, heating and cooling).

THE POWER OF CONTEXT

I am fascinated with the power of context. More and more I notice the effects that context can have on organizations and other kinds of human systems. Here are a few examples.

Effect of Office Design on Communication or Vice Versa

One of my clients was the head of development for a systems company. While conducting an organizational assessment for him, my partner and I noticed that the company's office space was arranged peculiarly. My client's group shared the office space with Customer Support, Marketing, Production, and Finance. The one-story office building was a maze of corridors, rooms, and offices. There were only a few windows and those were in the executive offices.

There were lots of doors, some of which could be locked to keep others out. One door even had a sign on it that read, "This door will be locked from 2:00 PM until 4:00 PM each day. Please do not knock as no one will answer." That door had a cipher lock on it. Only the manager behind the door and members of his group knew the combination.

We also noticed that there were multiple ways to get from point A to point B in the building. So if one wanted to avoid a certain person, one could always find a path around that person. There seemed to be a remarkable similarity between the physical layout of the building and the way people in the organization did or did not communicate with one another. This pattern of communication was especially evident among the executive team. I asked if the building was that way when they first occupied it. I was told no, "it was much more open when our company moved here. The walls, doors, locks, and corridors were added later."

Effect of Time Format on a Critical Routine

I was conducting a project retrospective for a client. One of the significant events during the project was a repeating system failure at a client site during a new installation, which was disabling the client's business. The defect that caused the failure had been very difficult to trace. The developer spent several days going over code and running diagnostics.

The failure was finally traced to a routine that initiated several shut-down procedures that had to be executed in a precise order. The routine was supposed to launch at midnight each night. The developer had been staring at the defect for several days without noticing that the code in the offending routine contained a test scheduled to execute at 2400 hours. Of course, there is no such time in the computer's clock. The clock proceeds from 2359 hours to 0000 hours. Thus, the routine never executed; instead, the system would crash. The developer had come from a different context—the military context—where midnight is often referred to as 2400 hours.

Effect of Explicit Agreement on Project Outcome

My partner and I were called in to do a large enterprise resource planning (ERP) project review for a client. One of the ERP modules had been implemented after two years and $20 million. The users revolted. So many errors were being produced that payroll had to be manually kludged.

After a few interviews, we learned that the project sponsor, who was also the chief financial officer for the client, had given strict orders to the project director to hold to the schedule and cost. The project director did that. In that context, the project director had been successful. We asked the sponsor and project director how quality had fit into their plans. It hadn't. They certainly got what they managed—schedule and cost. However, quality was a part of the project context that the sponsor failed to notice until it was too late.

I might easily have titled this book *Congruent Project Leadership*. Virginia Satir's congruence model, with its self, other, and context components, is very much integrated with my ideas of powerful project leadership. However, self, other, and context, while themes, do not explain all of what I mean by powerful project leadership. There is more—much more. Each of the three parts of this book, Leading Yourself, Leading Others, and Shaping Your Project's Context, contains chapters that offer additional models, techniques, and ideas to round out my meaning of powerful project leadership.

Part One
LEADING YOURSELF

Powerful project leadership begins with you. The ability to lead yourself is your most powerful resource when you are leading others in project work. If you do it well, you can increase your ability to lead others and resolve difficult project problems.

The idea of leading yourself is like the idea that a rescuer has to take care of himself first so that he can then rescue others. Leading yourself means keeping your "self" in the picture. Leading yourself also means keeping yourself strong by practicing good self-care—diet, exercise, rest, stress management. Keep yourself strong and in the picture so that you can use yourself in powerful ways to help your project.

You keep your "self" in the picture by being aware of both your internal feelings and your external behavior. You act mindfully, not out of unknown or unconscious reasons, even when you feel stuck, angry, afraid, hopeless, surprised, panicky, embarrassed, attacked, alone, sabotaged, confused, stupid, or incompetent. When you act mindfully, you process available information and respond carefully instead of acting automatically without thinking. You consider both your own needs and the needs of others. Your actions seem appropriate given your current context. If you ignore your self, others, or context, then your ability to lead yourself and others and to resolve difficult project problems will diminish.

You consider both your own needs and the needs of others.
Your actions seem appropriate given your current context.

You do not have to gratify everyone's needs, only consider them. Leading yourself does not mean that your actions will be perceived as right or fair or that others will applaud you. Others may or may not like you or your actions, but they will notice the connection between what you say and what you do. Your messages will be straight: What you say and how you look on the outside match how you feel inside. When the two do not match, you give a double message and others don't know which to believe—your words or how you look and sound. For example, if you are mad as hell inside, but you tell me you are not, I may not know whether to believe your words or your red face and set jaw. Straight messages are easier to trust. Leading yourself in this way will have subtle, positive effects on the attitudes and behavior of others.

The following are three stories based on real (though disguised) situations as related to me by some of my consulting clients and associates. In these stories, each leader was doing his or her best to deliver a successful project under difficult circumstances. Each made attempts to get help from a boss who could reasonably be expected to help. But all were ignoring one or more of the following: their own needs, the needs of others, or the appropriateness of their actions given their project's context. In various ways, these leaders were trying to lead others without their most powerful resource: their ability to lead themselves.

See if you can relate to any of these challenging situations.

A ROGUE PROJECT MANAGER?

Robert is a project director in the information technology (IT) services organization of a large corporation. His project is a multiyear, multimillion dollar ERP system project approaching go-live for a major component of that system.

Robert has a project manager reporting to him (one of four) for purposes of the project, but who reports functionally to another executive. Let's call her Alice. Her responsibility is the HR module, which includes payroll. Robert perceives Alice to be difficult to work with, and he is concerned about her module. She will not give him status reports on time. She always has an excuse for missing project team meetings.

The other three project managers coordinate their efforts with each other. They keep Robert informed. They do not know what Alice's team is doing and vice versa. She seems to be taking her team in a different direction from the other teams. Robert has tried talking with her directly about his concerns. She won't talk with him about what's happening. Robert has discussed this situation with Alice's functional boss. There has been no change that he can observe.

Finally, in desperation, Robert goes to the project's two senior executive sponsors. He presents his concerns regarding the apparent disconnection between

Alice's team and the other teams. Somehow these two executives don't perceive the problem to be important enough to show up on their radar screen. "It's just a personality issue," they say. "Work it out with her." As Robert leaves, he says, "You bet." Inside, Robert is feeling alone and unsupported. His stomach is in a knot. He sucks up all the responsibility because this is what he does when he does not know what else to do. He does this unconsciously.

Robert tries to keep the other three teams informed the best he can. The ERP system is tightly integrated and the modules are interdependent. This requires close coordination among the project teams. Alice continues to act as though she does not report to Robert. Her team becomes isolated and disconnected from the rest of his project teams. Her team literally splits off from the other teams and becomes a separate project. Robert gives up and lets them.

Several months later, after go-live, the impact of this problem becomes very visible. The lack of coordination between Alice's team and the technical infrastructure team results in serious execution and data errors. User confidence is severely damaged because users were not prepared for the required changes in how they do their work. Some of the expected functionality of the implemented system is not available. This surprised users because they were not involved in testing the functionality. All these impacts can be directly related to increasing project cost by millions of dollars. There is plenty of blame, most of it finding its way to Robert.

What was happening?

Robert had gradually lost his ability to lead himself. He was not aware of, nor was he using, his own power. He was stuck. His needs for information, structure, and project oversight were not being considered in any way that he could notice. Letting Alice's team run wild was neither respectful nor caring of any of the four teams, the users, or the executive sponsors. It was also not caring of himself. It was an unconscious, automatic response, not a mindful one. Robert's behavior was inappropriate for the project's context—tightly integrated software and data among modules, which required users to change how they do their work. Such tight integration and business process changes required the four project teams to coordinate their efforts closely.

What might Robert have done to act more powerfully? He could have responded by:

1. *Focusing the team structure and communication issues for the executives and user management* by presenting them as project risks instead of complaints about Alice. He could have included the severity, probability, and impact of the risks as well as prevention strategies and mitigation tactics. This would have acknowledged both Robert's needs and the needs of the executives, us-

ers, and project teams. It would have been appropriate given the project's context to bring attention to serious project risks.

2. *Asking the executives to support him in replacing Alice* with another project manager (since the risks were already occurring).

INFORMATION DEADLOCK?

Jackie is a new software development project manager in a computer manufacturing company. She has 15 years of experience with design and coding. This is her first development project as a manager. Jackie's five-person development team is inexperienced, with the exception of one person whom she perceives is a prima donna and often holds the team hostage. Jackie's manager is her long-time friend. The two of them have been together for years through various reorganizations and mergers.

Recently Jackie's company was bought by another, larger company. The new company's culture is very different from the old company's culture. Her team's customer is located in a different state where the new company's headquarters is located. Her team's software has to integrate with software from another team that also resides in the new headquarters.

Jackie's team is to develop proprietary software, which is vital to the new company's competitive edge. Her team has been given a deadline that was not derived from any estimates, but was instead based on "market timing." Jackie's team is expected to commit to the deadline. The software specifications change weekly—but the deadline does not. To make matters worse, the development environment her team must use is still in development itself and technical information about it is scarce. Communication is difficult between Jackie's team and the team with which they have to integrate.

Teleconferences are frustrating at best. The team on the other end of the line waits for her team to ask questions. But her team doesn't know enough to know what questions to ask. When someone on Jackie's team finally does ask a question, the response is often, "We'll have to check with our management first; we aren't sure if we can tell you that."

Jackie has asked her manager to intervene to help get the information her team needs. Her manager had a good reputation in the old company. He tries, but he also meets with resistance. Meanwhile, the clock is ticking. Jackie's communication is strained now with both her team and her manager/friend. Her manager becomes critical of her management style and offers to get her some professional coaching. Inside, Jackie feels incompetent and blames management for putting her in this impossible situation. Her neck and shoulders are noticeably tense. She refuses to commit. Her team has virtually stopped working, claiming "We can't do our work because they won't give us the information we need. There is no way we can meet the deadline."

What was happening?

Jackie resisted the pressure to commit to what she felt was an impossible deadline. On the surface, this might look like she is aware of and using her own power. But her resistance was actually a blaming test of wills based on her emotional response—feeling incompetent. Her resistance was not based on a credible analysis of anyone's needs or the project's context. There was no project plan or risk management plan.

What might Jackie have done to act more powerfully? She could have responded by:

1. Producing a project plan based on a credible work breakdown structure and estimates. Respecting management's deadline, this plan could clearly show which functionality and features can be produced by the deadline.
2. Producing a risk management plan that clearly identifies the information deadlock as a serious project risk. This plan could include any other risks associated with an unstable development environment.
3. With the help of her boss if necessary, presenting both plans to an executive sponsor who is high enough organizationally to make decisions for both Jackie's team and the other team. She would have been able to tell the executive sponsor what she wanted to do about the information deadlock and what she wanted the sponsor to do to support her.

A PROBLEM EMPLOYEE?

Terry is the manager of a small software group that produces specialty proprietary software for the financial services industry. Terry, his team, and his boss were all acquired intact when a large computer company bought their post-IPO startup company.

Terry has three underperforming employees and three performing employees. He had worked with one of the underperformers, let's call him Ralph, for a long time as a peer. During that time, Ralph had been a good performer. Now Terry is Ralph's boss, and recently Terry has been disappointed with Ralph's performance. Ralph is a huge puzzle to Terry. Ralph won't talk with Terry seriously about his performance. Terry knows he needs to do something about Ralph. He has considered firing Ralph. However, he knows that Ralph has a potentially large sum of money coming in stock options and Terry doesn't want Ralph to lose those options. Terry once thought he had a deal with Human Resources to buy Ralph out, but HR has recently been reorganized. The new HR decision-maker won't approve the same deal.

Terry counts heavily on his three performing employees. Without these three employees, his group's productivity would fall below zero. They keep him afloat, but also prolong his avoidance in dealing with Ralph. They are younger, less experienced, and their skills are still developing, but Terry makes allowances for them—perhaps too many.

Terry really needs help dealing with Ralph. Terry's boss is very busy and hard to reach. When Terry finally corners his boss for two minutes, his boss is reading and responding to his email while Terry talks. Without eye contact, his boss says, "I have complete confidence in you, Terry, and I know you will figure this out. Anything else?" Terry is disappointed by his boss' response. He turns and leaves mumbling, "Guess not." Inside, Terry feels abandoned, stuck, and hopeless. He notices he sighs a lot lately.

What was happening?

Terry was stuck holding himself hostage. His need to deal with Ralph's performance was being overshadowed by his desire for Ralph to get his stock options. The need and desire had created a dilemma for Terry. To Terry, the dilemma felt like this: Either he deals with Ralph's performance problem or he does not. If Terry deals with Ralph's performance problem, then Ralph will lose his stock options—an unpleasant choice. If Terry does not deal with Ralph's performance problem, then he knows he is not doing his job as a manager and he feels incompetent—an equally unpleasant choice. He has allowed his dilemma to take him out of the picture, so to speak. Because he was not using his power, he was unable to act appropriately given his project's context. That is, he was not able to be straight with anybody—his boss, Ralph, or his three less-experienced employees.

What might Terry have done to act more powerfully? He might have looked for ways to defeat the dilemma such as:

- Reframing the need and desire so that they are no longer "either–or." For example, Terry might have investigated with HR other ways to deal with Ralph's performance problem that do not threaten Ralph's stock options.
- Adding a third, fourth, or fifth choice to break the binary trap.

Robert, Jackie, and Terry are not bad leaders because they were not able to lead themselves in these difficult situations. It is entirely human for this to happen to any or all of us. It has happened to me many times. I cannot promise that leading yourself will result in a perfect project. But I have seen projects that have gone better and been more successful because the leaders were learning to lead themselves, even under difficult circumstances.

Chapter 1
THE ZEROETH STEP

As noted in the Introduction, one essential concept of leading yourself is considering both your own needs and the needs of others. Your actions seem appropriate given your current context.

This might sound reasonable. But to consider my needs, I first have to know what they are. I also need to know the needs of others. How can I do this? And who are these others? How can I tell if my actions make sense given my project's current context? What *is* my project's current context?

The zeroeth step is a technique designed to help you focus on those questions before you officially kick off your project—before the inevitable pressure sets in. The zeroeth step is time you take just for you. Typical goals of the zeroeth step are self-awareness, balance, and self-direction. On the list of what to do differently next time, project leaders for whom I have conducted retrospectives frequently write "take more time for myself in the beginning to get centered, be clear about what I need from my project, and make a plan for myself." This observation is what led me to develop the zeroeth step. It is a technique you can use to prepare yourself to lead a new project or one already in progress. It is like a health spa for your mind and spirit. It gives you the edge you need to do your best.

To get the most out of the zeroeth step, you will need to understand the following concepts:

- The paradox of starting before you start
- The shaping effect of the paradox
- The paradox applied
- Taking the zeroeth step
- Taking it again.

THE PARADOX OF STARTING BEFORE YOU START

Is it really possible to start before you start? If so, will that amplify your leadership effectiveness? The answers are yes and yes. The first step is, of course, the first step, but it is not necessarily the start. For example, my first step in writing this book was to write a book proposal for the publisher. But I started "writing" this book years before that. Years of writing articles and collecting notes in folders from my consulting and training experiences went by before the idea of writing a book bubbled up to my conscious mind. When the book idea finally popped, it was not this book, although it eventually morphed into this book.

The paradox of the zeroeth step is a good reminder that a lot happens before the first step. For example, you may attend a lot of meetings. These might be project meetings, design meetings, issue resolution meetings, school meetings, church meetings, or family meetings. Recall a recent meeting you attended. When did that meeting start? You might be tempted to say, "today at 1:30 PM," or some other response naming a day, date, and time. I'll bet that the meeting actually started before "today at 1:30 PM." If any participants arrived early, it is likely that they started talking with each other. When my clients pay me to observe meetings, I show up early and quite often there is already a meeting going on before the meeting. These pre-meetings are usually much more interesting and informative than the scheduled meetings.

Other activities that often occur prior to the scheduled start of the meeting include:

1. Someone scheduled a room for the meeting.
2. Someone solicited agenda items in advance for the meeting.
3. Someone prepared a presentation to deliver at the meeting.
4. Someone completed an outstanding action item to report.

What is so important about this? The meeting is being shaped, perhaps inadvertently, by all these activities—not just the meeting outcomes, but the meeting processes as well. By meeting processes, I mean how agendas are set, how decisions are made, how leadership is shared, how conflict is resolved, and how time is managed.

THE SHAPING EFFECT OF THE PARADOX

How does shaping work? Consider how the choice of meeting room can shape the meeting. The configuration, size, number of chairs, size and shape of the table, windows, lighting, ventilation, and visual aids in the room affect how the meeting is conducted. I observed a meeting once that was conducted in a room that had just been painted and new carpet had been laid. There were no windows in the room. The air was practically unbreatheable from paint and carpet glue fumes. No other room was available. It was a quick meeting and nothing was accomplished. That meeting was definitely shaped by the room. The person who scheduled the room did not know about the fumes and did not know to ask. Had she asked, I'm sure she would not have accepted the room and would have scheduled another. That choice would have shaped the meeting in a different way.

Shaping happens all the time, whether it is intentional or inadvertent. Once you realize this, you can intentionally shape all kinds of processes. You may not be able to shape a specific outcome, but with practice you can shape the process so that you increase your chances of getting a specific outcome.

You may not be able to shape a specific outcome, but you can shape the process so that you increase your chances of getting a specific outcome.

THE PARADOX APPLIED

The underlying paradox of the zeroeth step applies to most endeavors involving people and ideas, including projects. The value of knowing this is that you can start shaping processes and outcomes before the project starts, or reshaping them as the project progresses. You do that by:

- Becoming clearer about your own needs
- Identifying others who are affected so you can find out their needs
- Understanding the context of your project.

Preparing yourself to lead a project is not a discrete event. It is a continual process of checking and rechecking your own needs. Projects are dynamic. Your preparation needs to be dynamic too. Your project's needs will change, as will your needs.

With projects, "others" refers to the project community. The project community comprises people affected by the project: users, sponsors, customers, vendors, project teams, operations, customer support, and you. Understanding the project context means identifying the purpose and scope of the project, time constraints, any technical infrastructure required by the project, physical plant and facilities, methodologies, tools, policies, procedures, funding, and regulatory and legal requirements.

TAKING THE ZEROETH STEP

The zeroeth step is a journey inward—a journey inside you, a reflection, a private interview with yourself. When you are faced with leading a new project, it is natural to have many feelings about it. Even if the project is already in progress, it is new to you and you are new to the project. This is true whether you choose the project or it chooses you.

The zeroeth step will help you become aware of your feelings and keep you in the picture. It will help you think about what to investigate as you prepare yourself to lead a project: your own needs, the needs of others in the project community, and the project context.

Find a quiet place and try to put yourself in a reflective state of mind and body. Sit comfortably with both feet on the floor. Take a couple of deep breaths. Clear your mind of the things that may be distracting you, pulling you this way or that. You clear your mind by acknowledging the distractions, honoring them as important, and letting them fade for now, knowing that you can come back to them in a while.

Ask yourself the following questions, which are grouped into self, other, and context categories. Give yourself plenty of time. Do not rush yourself. Write your answers on paper or in a journal. When you are finished, you may be surprised by how much information you have collected about yourself. Some of the information may seem new to you. Some may seem familiar. Some of it may capture important questions and assumptions you want to check out further.

Questions about Self

What feelings are surfacing for me now as I think about leading this project?

Your feelings are where you get your juice—your energy. Excitement might give you one kind of energy. Fear might give you another kind of energy. You can have both at the same time. For some people, feeling scared might be a negative energy. For others, it might be a positive energy. For example, when I'm feeling scared about a new opportunity, that is a positive thing because experience tells me that it usually means I am going to learn something important. Allow this question to help you identify as many feelings as you can name. If you have trouble naming feelings, consider the following list. You may recognize some of these feelings.

The Big Four: mad, glad, sad, scared

More feelings: Angry, ashamed, bewildered, competent, confident, confused, depressed, embarrassed, empty, enraged, excited, exhausted, frightened, frustrated, furious, guilty, happy, helpless, hopeless, incompetent, joy-

ful, overwhelmed, paralyzed, relaxed, stressed, stunned, stupid, vulnerable, worried.

You do not have to DO anything with the feelings for now—just notice them and jot them down. Also jot down what it is like to be this aware of your feelings.

What do I hope can happen for me during this new project?

Some of us learned not to hope for something good for ourselves, or not to waste hope on something that is not likely to happen. If this is true for you, please resist your temptation to avoid this question. Allow this question to help you tease out your hopes. Remember, this is a private interview. No one has to know.

Hope
Is a weaver.
She is not much of a talker.
Sometimes she is so quiet
You hardly know
She's around.

If you tell her your desires,
She will weave them
Into a wonderful map.

Faith,
Her sister
Will paint silver compass points
On your map and
Start you
In the right direction.

If you can't think of anything to hope for, here are few possibilities that may trigger your thoughts:

- Learn something new like a technology, tool, or method
- Work with a specific individual
- Don't work with a specific individual
- Do it differently this time, not making the same mistakes
- Demonstrate your skill
- Stretch yourself (bigger scope or more complex)
- Take a rest, play it safe.

If you still cannot think of anything to hope for yourself, perhaps you should consider passing on this project. Without such hopes, you may find it difficult to be excited about your project.

What do I hope can happen for my organization?

It may be easier to direct your hopes toward something abstract, like your organization. Your "organization" can be your team, your department, or even your company. Perhaps this project will provide an opportunity:

- For your team to work together again because you all enjoyed the previous project so much
- To repair relationships damaged during the previous project
- For your department to be recognized for helping your company successfully penetrate a new market
- For your users to acknowledge your team's contribution to a smooth implementation
- For your customers to increase their business with your company, and recommend your company to their colleagues.

As you write down each hope, let yourself also begin to think about what it might take to make that hope come true. For example, what might it take for your users to acknowledge your team's contribution to a smooth implementation? What would "acknowledge" look or sound like? What would "smooth" mean to your users? Take a guess, then follow up later with some of your users and compare their answers to yours. Their answers can become goals to which your teams aspires.

What do I hope can happen for my customers?

This question is asking about your hopes for your customers—not your customers' hopes. At this time, you may not know your customers' hopes. Later, you may want to visit your customers and find out their hopes. Then, as you learn more about your customers' hopes, you can modify your list. Hopes are different from expectations. When talking with customers to find out their hopes, be sure to distinguish between hopes and expectations. For example, your customers may expect all the "must have" system functionality to work in the field. They may hope for a few "nice to have" functions as well. Inside, you may hope that for your customers as well. But be cautious about telling your customers your hopes for them. Your hopes can morph into their expectations before you know it!

If you do not know who your customers are, then it will difficult to have hopes for them (other than very general ones). If this is the case, then give yourself an action item to find out who your project's customers are. If you have multiple customers, each can have different hopes. Here are a few hopes for customers I have heard from project leaders:

- Surpass the anticipated advantage over their competitors.
- Save them twice the money they are expecting to save.
- Finish one month earlier with no reduction in functionality or quality.
- Make their transition to new business processes smoother because of the user training, help desk preparation, and on-line aids we will provide.

You may not be able to make any of your hopes for your customers come true, but by keeping an awareness of them, you can at least look for opportunities to try.

What worries or concerns do I have about leading this project?

This question invites you to explore any worried feelings you might have jotted down from the earlier question about feelings. For example, this project could be bigger than any you've led, or it could involve a technology new to you. Perhaps you know that one of your team members is going to be on medical leave for a month. You may worry about how to cover for him, or how to bring him up to speed when he returns. If you know that the customer of this project has a reputation for changing the project scope, you may be concerned about how to control scope change requests. Your answers aren't necessarily showstoppers—they are simply risks to be managed. Your list of worries could become the beginning of a risk management plan for your project.

What changes in my routine may be necessary to assist my organization and my customers with this project?

Your project may change your usual routine. Such changes are not uncommon. Some project leaders prefer not to think about this, believing that changes just go with the territory. They wait until a change happens and then try to deal with it. This question invites you to anticipate potential changes. If you take the opportunity to think about them in advance, you may be able to minimize their effects, or eliminate their effects altogether. Try to make your list without thinking ahead about your willingness to accommodate them. The accommodation question comes later. Here are some possible changes you may face:

- Your office hours
- Your office location
- How you spend your time
- Where you spend your time

- Who you spend time with
- Your priorities
- Your relationships with other people (boss, peers, associates, family)
- Your management style
- The tools you use
- Your performance objectives.

Which of these changes am I willing to accommodate?

As you look at your answers from the previous question, ask yourself which you are willing to accommodate—and which you may want to negotiate. For example, if your home is in Missouri, and your office must be in Ohio for a six-month project, you may want to negotiate a three day on-site, two day off-site arrangement. One way to arrange this would be to travel Sunday night to your office in Ohio, work there Monday through Wednesday, and travel home Wednesday night to Missouri. For those potential changes you want to negotiate, make notes to yourself about what you want and what your bottom line is for each.

What kind of support do I need for myself during this project?

This question relates in part to your list of worries and concerns. Think about what kind of support could help you deal with each worry. Support does not only have to be for worries. Support can also be for sustaining your positive energy and spirit. Kinds of support you may consider include:

- Periodic advice from a mentor
- A sounding board from an expert in the technology being used on your project
- Access to the project sponsors on a regular basis
- Access to a fitness center
- Access to your counterpart on interdependent projects.

Questions about Others

What perceived losses might individuals in this project's community resist?

Your project's community consists of all the individuals who can affect or be affected by your project. Your project could be perceived by some of those individuals as an unwelcome change to their routine. Unwelcome change often evokes feelings of loss. Kinds of loss that people sometimes feel include:

- Loss of relationships—A key individual to be assigned to your team has been taken against her wishes from another team where she felt very connected.

- Loss of power—A reorganization has resulted in another team's project being reassigned to your team. The parent organization of the other team is being significantly downsized and many of it projects are being reassigned to other teams in your parent organization.
- Loss of status—A management decision to outsource application development has put you in charge of the outsourcing project. You must work with the application development group and the application service provider. The future of the application development group is uncertain.

This question reminds you to anticipate the perception of loss. You can use your answers to prepare strategies for dealing with the losses—if they actually occur. The only way to know for sure is to check it out with the appropriate individual.

What kind of support do I imagine people on my team might want during this project?

The answers to this question will vary depending on the characteristics of the project. Consider a project that involves new technology, immature tools, more than 20 percent travel, and multiple geographically dispersed interdependent projects—and that is larger than any previously attempted. The following kinds of support could be imagined:

- Flexible work schedule
- Generous amounts of free food
- Prompt, reliable escalation process for handling cross-organizational problems
- Accurate, timely decisions that stick
- Some room to make mistakes
- Deadlines that acknowledge the use of new technology and immature tools
- Adequate time for training
- Free access to a fitness center
- Timely access to proper equipment and supplies
- Competent administrative services to handle travel arrangements.

Have I been clear enough with each executive sponsor about his/her time commitment and what specifically I need him/her to do so that the project can be successful?

Executives are busy individuals. Even when they are willing, it is difficult to get their time. Do not expect them to read your mind regarding what you want them to do. Being an executive sponsor is a part-time job, and many executives receive no formal education on how to be a sponsor. The clearer you can be in advance, the better your chances of getting what you need from your executive sponsor. Tell him or her in advance how much time you want and how frequently. If you want her attendance at project functions, let her know the dates and times involved so she can put them on her schedule. The further out calendar-wise and the more predictable, the better. For example, a project all-hands meeting the first Tuesday of every month from 3:00 PM to 4:00 PM. If you bring a decision to be made, tell her that you want her to make the decision. Give her the background, urgency, and importance, and let her know when you need the decision.

Who might be able to give me the support I need?

This is the second part of the earlier question, "What kind of support do I need for myself?" Add to your list whomever you think could give you that support. Later you will want to check with those individuals to find out if they will in fact give you the support you need.

Who are the people this project needs to please?

It is to your advantage to find out who these people are. Make contact with them and discover their expectations. You will need their support. Some of the people on your list might include:

- Yourself
- Project sponsors
- Customer (client or user management)
- System architect
- Marketing executives
- Product management executives
- Other project leaders who depend on your project's output.

Questions about Project Context

What lessons are available to me from past projects that I want to use on this project?

Patterns of success and failure on projects tend to find their way from the past into the present, and can become part of your project's current context. It is wise to learn as much as you can about the patterns of projects in your organization. In some project-oriented cultures, project retrospectives are a natural event in the life of a project. In such cultures, a project plan includes a line item and allocates time for a retrospective at the conclusion of the project. The documented lessons learned from a retrospective typically consist of lists: what worked, what didn't, and what to do differently next time.

A quick review of recent lessons from other projects may give you helpful hints for this project. If you are joining a project in progress, a project historian can be a valuable asset. If no such role exists, arrange to talk with the person who has been on the project the longest. Ask that person to fill you in on the history to date. The seeds of success and failure are there waiting to be discovered. This will be much more interesting than wading through stacks of status reports and issue logs, although some wading may be useful too. Be sure to create a project historian role if one does not already exist.

> *A project retrospective is a facilitated meeting during which project community members review a project that has ended. The purpose of a project retrospective is to examine in an explicit and public way what worked, what didn't, and how to do future projects better. The focus of a project retrospective is on learning from shared experiences, not on finding fault or placing blame.*

What are the expectations of the people this project needs to please?

This question goes with the earlier question about others, "Who are the people this project needs to please?" Their expectations are part of your project's current context. Discovering these expectations is essential to shaping your project's context for success. Why? Because it is nearly impossible to satisfy unknown expectations. (See Chapter 14 for details on how to do that.)

TAKING IT AGAIN

Preparing yourself to lead a project is not a discrete event. It is a continual process of checking and rechecking your own needs. Projects are dynamic. Your preparation needs to be dynamic too. Your project's needs will change, as will your needs. Do not hesitate to take the zeroeth step as often as you need. Here are a few hints that you may need to take it again:

- You start to feel overburdened, or like you want to run away and hide.
- You begin to feel that your project is out of control.
- A friend lets you know she is concerned about you, because you seem to be behaving out of character.
- You do not remember why you wanted to lead this project.
- The scope of your project changes significantly.

To recap:

- The zeroeth step can help you focus on important self, other, and context questions before the inevitable pressure of your project sets in.
- You can start your project before it starts by taking the zeroeth step.
- You can shape your project's process and outcomes by anticipating problems before they occur and making plans to avoid or minimize them.
- You can take the zeroeth step as often as you need. Preparing yourself to lead a project is not a discrete event. It is a continual process of checking and rechecking your own needs. This helps keep you in the picture and avoid losing yourself.

Try this:

1. Take the zeroeth step for yourself. Using the list of feelings you generated, record the strength of each feeling—strong or mild—and its direction—positive or negative. You might even try drawing this picture of your feelings in graphical form.
2. Arrive at your next meeting five minutes early. If your meeting culture is to start meetings five minutes after the scheduled time, then arrive at the scheduled meeting on time. Observe the meeting that is going on before the meeting. Jot down anything you notice that might be shaping the scheduled meeting. At the conclusion of the scheduled meeting, check your notes to see if you were correct.

Chapter 2

USING YOUR INTERNAL RESOURCES

Projects need many kinds of resources to be successful. Projects need skilled people, time, money, and tools, to name a few. Human beings—individuals—also need many resources to be successful. Fortunately, each of us is born with some very significant resources inside of us. In her inspiring poem, *The Five Freedoms,* Virginia Satir reminds us of the following internal resources:

- Thoughts
- Feelings
- Wants
- Voice
- Risk-taking.

The Five Freedoms[1]

The freedom to see and hear what is here,
instead of what should be, was, or will be
The freedom to say what you feel and think,
instead of what you should
The freedom to feel what you feel,
instead of what you ought
The freedom to ask for what you want,
instead of always waiting for permission
The freedom to take risks on your own behalf,
instead of choosing to be only "secure" and not rocking the boat

---

[1]Virginia Satir, et al., *The Satir Model, Family Therapy and Beyond* (Palo Alto: Science and Behavior Books, Inc. 1991), p. 62. Reprinted with permission.

Unlike external resources (money, for instance), which can come and go, our internal resources never leave us. They are our birthright. When we are aware of our internal resources and use them appropriately, we feel stronger and more capable. We are more able to make decisions in our own best interest. We are more capable of changing and growing in new directions when we choose to. We are not defeated when our external resources become scarce. This sense we have of our own strength and capability is sometimes called high self-esteem.

Our parents were our first teachers about our resources, strengths, capabilities, and self-esteem. Some were better teachers than others, and I truly believe that all did their best given their own capabilities. Regardless of how well we were taught, we can become disconnected from our internal resources or temporarily forget how to use them. When this happens, our effectiveness as a person falls short of what it could be. A powerful project leader is first an effective person—one who will use her internal resources to sustain her strength and capability so she can deal effectively with even the most challenging project situations.

Do not expect anyone to be glad or to give you an award for using your internal resources. In fact, sometimes doing so can be career-limiting. For example, some individuals who do not feel effective themselves may be intimidated by your effectiveness. These individuals may attempt to stall your career and you may not even know it. Some people may get angry with you, especially when you suddenly change and start using your resources. When they see you using yours, it could call into question how effectively they use theirs. Some who have forgotten how to use their internal resources may think, "What gives you the right to be strong and capable?" Even friends and family can get upset with you because your changing means they too might have to change.

You may have to settle for your own satisfaction with how you feel about yourself. In the end, this is the best reward anyway. You may want to look for career opportunities where you can thrive using your resources. The only people to applaud you may be others who fully use their own internal resources. They will recognize and appreciate the difficulty of what you are doing. They also know how rewarding it can be. For some, the increase in self-esteem outweighs the risk of losing a job or damaging a relationship.

THOUGHTS

Our thoughts are resources. Thoughts are private until we express them in some way, either verbally or nonverbally. Thoughts can amuse us. They can sadden us. They can frighten us. We can experience a wide range of feelings from just thinking our thoughts. Thoughts can lead us to action or just disappear without any action. We can invent solutions with our thoughts. We can invent problems too. We can compare and contrast our thoughts to the expressed thoughts of others. We can change our minds or not. Our ability to have our thoughts and think for ourselves is a very significant resource.

But we can lose touch with this resource. When we do not fully use our thinking resource, we limit ourselves. We give away some of our power. One way this can happen is when *we think what we should think instead of what we really think*. This might sound silly. But it happens more than you might imagine. All of us are capable of limiting ourselves this way. For example, some of us grew up in families where we were told what we should think and not think. It was like that in my family. In such families, the message a child can get is, "It doesn't matter what I think. I should always think what others want me to think. That is how to get along in the world." "Others" in this case means "big people"—adults we perceive to have power over us. After all, when we are small, we depend on big people for survival. As an adult in the workplace, the idea that we should think what others want us to think can sometimes carry over to people in authority—our boss, our boss' boss, and so on.

Our families did not intentionally do this to harm us. I believe that they had the best intentions, and did the best they could at the time, to try to protect us and teach us. They wanted to protect us from scary thoughts or thoughts that, if acted upon, might bring harm to us. These parents may not have known how to help us process our thoughts in healthy ways that allowed us to both have our thoughts and learn how to choose what to do with them. It may have been easier for them to just tell us what to think and not think. Unfortunately, the lessons we learned this way did not have automatic expiration dates. It may have escaped the notice of some parents to take their young adult aside and say, "It's time to think for yourself now."

FEELINGS

Our feelings are resources. Feelings are also private until we express them, either consciously or unconsciously. I am not talking about sensations such as those we feel through our skin, like heat or cold or pressure. I am talking about emotions. Feelings make life juicy. Feelings are not good or bad in and of themselves. Human beings have a large palette of feelings. There are the "big four" to which psychologists sometimes refer: mad, glad, sad, and scared. There are lots variations on these, in addition to scores of others.

Here are few more examples: angry, ashamed, bewildered, competent, confident, confused, depressed, embarrassed, empty, enraged, excited, exhausted, frightened, frustrated, furious, guilty, happy, helpless, hopeless, incompetent, joyful, overwhelmed, paralyzed, relaxed, stressed, stunned, stupid, vulnerable, worried.

Feelings arrive uninvited and unannounced as we experience the world around us. We cannot *not* have feelings. That is, we cannot control whether or when we have feelings, although some people may try to deny them or deflect them somewhere else. Some people may try to numb their feelings by self-medicating or by acting out in ways harmful to themselves or others. Such people are said to have difficulty coping when life meets them head on with all its opportunities and challenges.

How can we lose touch with this resource? When we do not acknowledge or use our feelings, we give away some of our power. We do not so much *lose* touch with our feelings, as *we never quite get in touch with them.* One way this can happen is similar to what happens to our thoughts. That is when *we feel what we should feel instead of what we really feel.* As with our thoughts, there are plenty of people who are ready, willing, and able to tell us what we should feel and not feel.

Many of us go through life befuddled by our feelings. Those of us befuddled may not have developed a working vocabulary for expressing our feelings. The K-12 education systems in the United States tend to focus on cognitive and motor development at the expense of affective (emotional) development. So unless our parents taught us how to talk about our feelings and what to do with them, we very likely grew into adulthood with very limited capability for dealing with them.

I only began to seriously explore my feelings and develop a vocabulary for expressing them at age 38. I am not saying that I had no feelings until then. I certainly have had them during my life, especially terror and shame. But I did not understand them, nor did I feel safe expressing them until my late thirties. I mention the intense feelings of terror and shame to make a point. Feelings are so important to each and every one of us. For example, I firmly believe that much of the violence in the world comes as a result of us not knowing how to handle our intense feelings, such as hate, rage, shame, and terror, safely. My friend and colleague Jean McLendon, a therapist and organization development consultant, helped me understand this in the following way:

> *The precursor [to intense feelings which can lead to violence] is our not understanding the basic nature of the vulnerabilities associated with our*

physical, emotional and spiritual needs and freedoms. Ignoring our basic needs makes us less resilient, less creative, and less able to connect and resolve conflicts of need. There are lots of points before hate, rage, shame, and terror that are opportunities for understanding, compassion and connection. If the opportunities are not acted on then the feeling states expand with intensity and require great skill to manage. If we would deal with embarrassment and humiliation we wouldn't have to live with shame, if we would deal more courageously with our needs for safety, fear need not become terror. Our unattended hurts over time foster hate. Our anger, left to fester and provoked moves towards rage.[2]

WANTS

Our wants are resources. All of us have wants. We all have the ability to ask for what we want. But some of us learned to wait for permission rather than ask. I have been told that this is "polite." Waiting for permission means you have to depend on someone else to give you permission. That implies that someone else needs to be able to read your mind to know you want something so they can give you permission to ask for it. That is a big burden to put on someone else. I suspect that people who wait for permission spend a lot of their lives waiting for permission that never comes. I know I did. Not because others do not want to give their permission, but because others might not realize that anyone is waiting for their permission.

How can we lose touch with this resource? Some of us have difficulty asking for what we want. I remember being told as a youngster, "You shouldn't ask for things you know you can't have." This may have been a message out of the Great Depression era, when lots of things were scarce for many people. In that context, perhaps it made sense. My most generous interpretation is that it was supposed to protect me from being disappointed. But somehow I internalized that message as, "I shouldn't *want* things I know I can't have." I traded disappointment for something else—low self-esteem. I began to question my worth—maybe I did not deserve to have certain things.

One of my great moments of personal growth was when I realized that it was okay for me to want things even though I might not get them. That was such a freeing moment for me because until then I spent an enormous amount of energy trying to *not want* things that I really wanted. I felt better about myself knowing that having or not having something was not a function of my worth. Of course, it is perfectly fine for me to want to be a billionaire and I deserve to be. It is not likely I will become one, however.

---

[2]Email conversation with Jean McLendon, June 21, 2001.

VOICE

Our voice is a resource. When I say "voice," I mean our ability to comment on what we see, hear, think, and feel. This includes all forms of expressing our voice, whether it is speaking, signing, writing, singing, painting, or other mediums. It is hard for some of us to comment on what we see and hear. We might be labeled a troublemaker. It is hard for some of us to say what we think and feel. Someone might not like what we think or how we feel. We might get criticized. Or fired. Sometimes it is dangerous—even life-threatening—to say what we think and feel. The first amendment guarantees our right to do so, yet sadly there are still places in the United States where one can be seriously injured or killed just for speaking one's mind.

We lose touch with this resource when *we see and hear only what we should instead of what is.* Another way is when we *say what we ought to say instead of what we really think and feel.* Where do we get the ideas about what we ought to see, hear, or say? Local culture can influence this. By local culture, I mean the system of beliefs and values that shapes behavior in a social system. A family is a social system. So is a church, a school, a company where you work, and so on. People are socialized by their culture to know what to see and hear and what to say and not say.

These rules are not written down anywhere. Each social system has its way of dealing with those who "break the rules." It may be just a look or a sigh or a gasp. Often no words need be spoken, yet the offender clearly gets the message. Privately, someone may take you aside and let you know that you have made a faux pas.

RISK-TAKING

Our ability to "go for it" is a resource. What this really means is taking risks in our own behalf. Some of us were taught to be careful: Be safe. Don't take a chance. The other extreme was the case in my immediate family. I never got that kind of message. My curiosity and adventuresome nature always got me into "situations," some dangerous. I do not recall ever being hobbled when it came to trying things. My parents were sometimes a little less watchful of me than safety might dictate. I once wandered off as a toddler from a barbecue picnic in the country. A passerby saw me standing on a narrow rock outcropping below which the rock wall dropped 150 feet into a large pool of water. I have no idea how I got there. I had found the rock quarry! I barely remember any of this—years later my parents told me they were "scared to death."

We lose touch with this resource when *we choose to be only secure and not rock the boat* instead of taking risks in our own behalf. How can this happen? When I was 20 years old I decided that I wanted to own my own business by the time I was 30. I was 45 when I started my own consulting business—15 years late. Why did I wait so long? I was the breadwinner for my then wife and two children. I had a good job and the thought of leaving it was very scary for me. Starting my own business felt risky at the time. It felt safer to keep a secure job with a predicable income and great health care benefits. I chose to be secure and not rock the boat. I rationalized that I was playing it safe for my family. The "security" was only an illusion, as I would eventually find out. I worked for that company for 26 years. Then I got laid off with no severance package. That is when I started my consulting business.

RESOURCEFULNESS ICONS

Resourcefulness icons are physical metaphors—objects—that represent some of our internal resources. Virginia Satir used metaphor extensively in her therapy and teaching work. She adopted several icons to represent a few internal resources—birth tools we all have—essential for maintaining self-esteem. The idea is that by holding or touching an icon, one may more easily access the resource that the icon represents. Virginia called the collection a self-esteem maintenance kit.[3] The tools themselves are universal, but the icons representing the tools may be cultural-, age-, or gender-biased.

The idea of this kit and its icons has been adapted and expanded upon by many of Virginia's students and associates. The following are some of my favorites. Feel free to adapt and add to these as you may. Make up your own kit. For example, my partner Eileen is fond of small polished stones with inspirational words etched into them. She put together a self-esteem maintenance kit using a set of stones with names and icons representing the birth tools. A few of the icons did not exist, so she negotiated with the business owner to create a few custom stones to complete two kits, one for her and one for me. From the same business owner she bought a beautiful small silk pouch to keep the kit in. The nice thing about the stone icons is that you can keep one you think you might need for a meeting or event in your pocket. No one knows you have the stone. When you need it, just reach into your pocket and be reminded of that resource. Other colleagues have created charm bracelets, necklaces, essential oils, and sculptures as their kits. There are so many creative ways to use the icons.

---

[3]Virginia Satir, et al., *The Satir Model, Family Therapy and Beyond* (Palo Alto: Science and Behavior Books, Inc. 1991), pp. 293-297.

Wishing Wand

The wishing wand represents our ability to have and to articulate our wishes and hopes. Our wishes and hopes often are a source of motivation. Holding the wishing wand in my hand is a physical reminder of my power to articulate my wishes and hopes. Sometimes I need this reminder to give me a little power boost. Use the wishing wand in combination with the other icons to boost your power even more.

Courage Stick

The courage stick represents our ability to activate our courage. Our courage empowers us to take action even when we know there will be difficulties. Sometimes we may need our courage to take a first little step, like asking for something we really want. Maybe I want to start a new relationship or end an existing one. Maybe I want to make a career change or run a marathon. Maybe I want to say no to something that does not fit, but I feel pressured to say yes. The courage stick is a physical reminder of my courage to go for something I really want—or to say no to something that does not fit.

Wisdom Box

The wisdom box represents our ability to connect with our deepest knowing about what fits for us. For me, the wisdom box is that small, still voice inside that tries to give me direction. Virginia believed that the wisdom box connects us to the wisdom of the universe.

Golden Key

The golden key represents our ability to open any door and check out new possibilities. Use your golden key to follow your curiosity into the unknown.

Detective Hat

The detective hat represents our ability to investigate and explore without judging. Use your detective hat whenever there is a puzzle, or a question, or an effort to understand. With the detective hat, you can ask the unaskable and speak the unspeakable in your search for truth.

Yes/No Medallion

The yes/no medallion represents our ability to choose with integrity. On one side the medallion says "yes"; on the other side it says "no." Both are loving words. Use your medallion to keep you strong in your integrity by saying your real yes and your real no. My real yes is the yes I say when I feel yes on the inside. My real yes carries with it my awareness and conscious choice to say, "Thank you for asking. Yes. What you ask fits for me at this time." My real no is the no I say when I feel no on the inside. My real no carries with it my awareness and conscious choice to say, "Thank you for asking. No. What you ask does not fit for me at this time." When you say yes and you feel no, or when you say no and you feel yes, you erode your integrity and weaken your self-esteem.

One More Icon: The Heart

My colleague Jean McLendon, who worked closely with Virginia Satir for many years, added the heart to the icons Virginia identified. The heart represents our ability to have and share our feelings. Feelings are information for us about what is happening inside ourselves. Our feelings are what enable us to make a heart connection with another person, should we choose to do that. By heart connection I mean a mutual sharing of something significant at the feeling level such as joy or sadness, or love. We could not truly care for others, causes, or ourselves, without heart. It is heart that allows us to give our most generous and helpful interpretation of the actions and words of others. In other words, we look for positive intentions. When we cannot access our heart, we sometimes give our worst and malicious interpretation—we assume malicious intentions.

PERSONAL EFFECTIVENESS APPLIED TO PROJECTS

Up to this point, the emphasis has been on being a more effective person by using your internal resources. Now let us look at how using your internal resources can help you be a more effective project leader. It may not be obvious how a project leader could use her internal resources in project situations. The following table contains several examples of project situations and the resources that might be used in those situations.

Situation	Resources to Use
Responding to pressure with what you really think. For example, your boss asks you privately what you think the chances are that your project will make its next major milestone on time. You think it is almost guaranteed to be a week late. Before you can answer, your boss says, "We absolutely cannot miss this milestone. We are going to make it, right?"	Use your own independent thoughts. Use your voice to say what you think instead of what you imagine your boss wants to hear. Use the courage stick and the medallion to say your real yes or no. Use your wisdom box to offer your boss tradeoffs or alternative solutions.
Choosing again to do something different based on new information. For example, suppose some new product requirements present themselves. You estimate that the new requirements will lengthen the project schedule and increase both cost and risk. On the other hand, accommodating the new require-ments will make it possible for the product to penetrate a previously overlooked market, and give your company a competitive advantage. You fear being held to the original approved schedule and resources. A part of you wants to resist the new requirements and stick with the original approved schedule and budget. You want to help the company, and you know you will have to negotiate for additional schedule time and resources to protect yourself.	Once decided, we sometimes think we must stick with our decision no matter what. Use your medallion to choose again when you get new information. Your wisdom box can tell you what fits for you regarding the new information. Your detective hat can help you investigate and understand the opportunities and risks associated with adding the new requirements. Choosing again may require courage to negotiate for more time and resources. Use the courage stick along with your voice to say what you think and feel and ask for what you want.
Asking for a "time out" when your peers seem to be shouting, "Shut up and keep rowing!" Suppose your team of peers is responsible for selecting the vendor to provide an	Your heart can keep you in touch with your feelings—worried, frus-trated, or scared—when others are saying, "Don't worry." Honor your wants by using your golden key and

Situation	Resources to Use
ERP system for your company. Electronic workflow is a must-have requirement. Only one vendor has been able to demonstrate this capability. Your peers are pressing you hard for your vote to select that vendor. They want to get the selection over quickly so they can get on with the project. The selection is already two weeks overdue. You are hesitating because during the demo the sales representative said, "This system is almost identical to the one you would be purchasing." You want the team to hold off on the decision until you can verify that the system to be purchased will provide electronic workflow. Your peers are frustrated with you and say, "Don't worry. You saw the demo with your own eyes and the workflow satisfies us."	courage stick to help you ask for "time out" to consider other possibilities. Use your voice to say what you really think and feel no matter how much pressure you feel to go along with the group-think.
Tossing your name in the hat for that radical career change opportunity. You have been a programmer your entire 16-year career. Your organization is forming a new architecture review function. The head of that function has posted open positions for an architecture review team. You feel ready for the challenge and although it seems risky, you know the senior management of the company is driving many process improvements. You interpret the formation of this architecture review function as evidence of their commitment. You decide to go for it.	Consult your wisdom box to know in your deepest way of knowing that the opportunity fits for you. Use the heart for caring enough about yourself to even consider it. Use the courage stick to ask for what you want. Take a risk in your own behalf and go for it. Use the wishing wand to express your hopes and wishes for yourself in going for it.

Situation	Resources to Use
Calling attention to the *dead elephant* in the middle of the room that everybody is ignoring. It's the problem everybody knows exists, but nobody will confront. For example, suppose you are a systems architect. You and a group of developers have been very happy with the work of a four-person business analyst team so far. Suddenly, a new analyst is brought in from another firm and put in charge of that team. He was personally recruited by a senior executive of your company. The new analyst starts taking the requirements work of that team of analysts and abstracting it so much that it starts to look like a design instead of requirements. You and the developers and the system architect now begin to have difficulty verifying that the software and architecture will satisfy the user requirements. You have privately spoken with the four analysts and they are so frustrated that two of them are considering quitting the company. No one has come forward to confront the *dead elephant*. You decide to do it yourself.	Use the courage stick to face the situation. Use the detective hat to ask questions in an effort to understand and comment nonjudgmentally on the situation. There might be a logical reason that the new leader of the business analyst group is designing instead of documenting requirements. Use the courage stick to access your courage to confront the situation congruently with regard for yourself, others, and the context. Use the medallion to say your real yes and real no, keeping your integrity strong. Use the golden key to help you explore possible solutions. Use your heart to give the most generous and helpful interpretation to the words and actions of all involved.

To recap:

- Unlike external resources, our internal resources—thoughts, feelings, wants, voice, risk-taking—never leave us. Jean McLendon points out that we may not be aware of them, we may feel we have lost them, or perhaps we are not sure we have ever been introduced to them.[4]
- When we are aware of our internal resources and use them appropriately, we feel stronger and more capable. Our self-esteem is higher.
- The resourcefulness icons—wishing wand, courage stick, wisdom box, golden key, detective hat, yes/no medallion, and heart—can be physical reminders of our resources. When we hold an icon in our hand or picture it in our mind, we can be physically reminded of the corresponding resource we have inside us.

Try this:

1. Create your own self-esteem maintenance kit. Do not limit yourself to the icons presented in this chapter. Choose symbols and resources that have significance for you.
2. Which internal resources are you most in touch with? Least in touch with? Which do you use most?
3. Think of a current project situation that you struggle with. Which of your internal resources could help you deal with that situation? How might you apply them to that situation?

[4]Handwritten feedback from Jean McLendon, July 15, 2001.

Chapter 3

DEALING WITH A DIFFICULT PERSON

You know who they are, those difficult people with whom you unfortunately have to work. There is Joe, who never seems to accept responsibility for the poor quality of his work or for not completing his work on time. According to him, he is a victim of uncooperative others and circumstances. There is Amy, who always seems to know what is best for everybody. She seems obligated to tell you what you should do. You could no doubt add to this list with your own examples. Do you ever wish you could deal with these "difficult people" more effectively? If you could, think how much more effective you would be at leading your project.

I believe that there is no such thing as a difficult person. There are, however, lots of people with whom I have difficulty. That does not necessarily mean that they are difficult people. "NOT!" you may say. Ten years ago I might have agreed with you. But I have learned some things about myself since then that have changed my mind. One thing I learned is that the difficulty is often more about me than about them.

When you label someone a difficult person, it is easy to project most—if not all—the responsibility for the difficulty onto that person. When you do that, you give up some of the power you need to deal with him or her effectively. Taking responsibility for your difficulty with such people helps you keep your power.

To make the shift in your thinking from "difficult person" to "person I have difficulty with," it will be useful to understand:

- That "difficult" is an interpretation
- How "filters" play into your interpretation
- What the "troubles and trophies" of filters are

- How to become aware of your filters
- How to use your awareness of filters to change how you respond.

"DIFFICULT" IS AN INTERPRETATION

During the past 10 years, I have been learning ideas, models, tools, and techniques from the counseling body of knowledge. One thing I have learned is how our intake from others and our responses to others are filtered. Intake means what we take in through our five senses: sight, sound, smell, touch, and taste. Intake includes the words we hear from others and their tone of voice, but not our interpretation of the words and tone of voice. Intake is not inherently "difficult." For example, you ask me, "What time is it?" I hear your words, what—time—is—it. I see your face. It looks relaxed. Your tone of voice seems unremarkable, neither loud nor soft.

Intake is merely words, sounds, and expressions. Our interpretation of the intake is what makes it "difficult" or not. I could interpret from your question that you mean I am late. I could feel criticized. The simplified diagram below illustrates how behavior originating from another person goes through various filters and can then be *interpreted* by me as difficult.

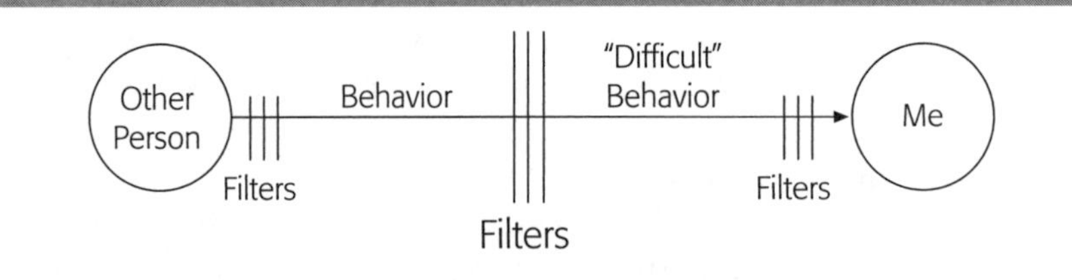

"Response" is how and what we express to others when we respond. Response includes our words, body language, facial expression, and tone of voice. Sometimes our response is not the same as what we think or feel inside. When that happens, we are filtering our response.

TYPES OF FILTERS

We all have filters. A filter is a device that lets some things, but not others, pass through. A coffee filter lets water, but not coffee grounds, pass through. A filter in a furnace lets air pass through while trapping dust, pollen, and other impurities. For our purposes, I use "filter" to refer to devices that affect how we perceive others (intake filters) or respond to others (response filters). Our filters may be completely out of our awareness. For example, I may know that I get annoyed by people who are not precise with the words they choose. But I might not think of that as a filter—it is the *people who don't use words with precision* filter.

Some perceived behaviors are acceptable to us, while others are not. Those we do not accept can be difficult for us to handle. We might label those behaviors difficult. We might go further. For example, when confronted with behavior I interpret as difficult, I might be tempted to label not just the behavior, but also the person, difficult. I might want to get away or punish that person in some way, but my response filters can cause me to respond in a more generous way, such as trying to find a positive intention behind the behavior.

As individuals, we have both intake filters and response filters. Some filters can be both. Additionally, environmental filters (such as noise) can affect our intake. To illustrate what I mean, here are some examples of my filters.

Intake Filters

- *Do what you say you will do* filter—If you seem to consistently fail to do what you tell me you'll do, this filter might kick in. This type of behavior is difficult for me to tolerate. Eventually, I will find it hard to take you seriously. Taken to extremes, I may try to avoid you altogether. I think this may be a value of mine: "I should do what I say I am going to do. So should everyone else." This filter helps me manage my expectations of others' dependability—at least my idea of dependability.
- *Loud, aggressive people* filter—If I perceive you shouting me down and telling me that my needs don't matter, this filter might kick in. This type of behavior is difficult for me to tolerate. Eventually, I'll refuse to be in same room with you. This filter helps me maintain my self-esteem.
- *Putting on hats* filter—If you remind me of someone from my past, I might start interacting with you as though you were that other person. I may be completely unaware I'm doing this. In essence, I am putting a "hat" on you. If my expectations of you are filtered by that hat, good or bad, that can lead to trouble. For example, I did not get along well with my fifth-grade teacher and thought she was mean and cruel to me. If you remind me of my fifth-grade teacher, I might avoid you or become very short with you. This may be very confusing for both of us.
- *Environmental* filters—Have you ever tried to have a conversation on a cell phone with a poor connection? In a similar way, I may not receive all the intake due to noise or other distractions. The meaning of a message can sometimes turn on one word, which, if missed,

can result in a miscommunication. Even when my ears hear all the words, I can still sometimes hear one or more words inaccurately. For instance, you may say "can't," but I hear "can," perhaps because I'm expecting to hear "can." Also, when communicating with people whose primary language is not the same as mine, I can be confused by accents and choice of words.

- *Personality type* filters—These can affect how I perceive others. For example, in meetings, people with a preference for introversion[1]—like me—may find it difficult to get a word in edgewise with people who have a preference for extraversion.[2] To "extraverts" it may look like the "introverts" aren't participating. To "introverts" it may look like the "extraverts" are participating too much. Both are merely interpretations. Generally, introverts process their thoughts inside before speaking. There is a silent pause while the processing takes place. When an introvert finishes processing his thoughts, he then speaks. Generally, extraverts process their thoughts outside by talking them out. There is little, if any, silent pause for processing.
- *You must be stupid* filter—Sometimes this filter kicks in when I cannot make any sense of what I perceive your behavior to be. This is more likely to happen when I am tired, ill, upset, or not feeling good about myself. I might hear myself say inside my head, "Stupid!"
- *You are trying to screw me* filter—This filter might kick in when I perceive that you are doing or saying something just to hurt me. As with the *you must be stupid* filter, this can happen when I am tired, ill, upset, or not feeling good about myself. When I am feeling at my worst, it is easier to jump to this worst-case interpretation.
- *Generous interpretation* filter—This is the filter I use when I am able to give a generous interpretation to what I perceive you are doing or saying. When I am at my best, I can more easily use this filter instead of the *you are trying to screw me* or *you must be stupid* filter. I still may be confused by my perception of your behavior, but I try to look for a positive intention behind it.

Response Filters

- *Seen as helpful* filter—I want to be seen as helpful. I usually try to respond to people in a helpful way. My understanding of what

---

[1]Attitude descriptor from the Myers-Briggs Type Indicator, a registered trademark of Consulting Psychologist Press, Inc., Palo Alto, CA.

[2]Ibid.

is helpful has changed dramatically over the past 10 years. I used to inflict my help randomly on people whether they wanted it or not. Now I know much more about how to be a helpful person. At least I first ask if any help is desired. If the answer is no, I respect that. If the answer is yes, then I try to find out what would be helpful rather than assuming I know. This filter gets me in trouble sometimes with people who expect me to read their minds to find out what would be helpful. It also keeps me out of trouble with people who get offended by unsolicited help.

- *Don't celebrate too much or too soon* filter—When I really go for something and finally get it, this filter keeps me from expressing my joy, happiness, or excitement. I'm afraid that if I do express my joy, the wonderful thing I got will go away, disappear, or be taken back. I think I got this filter during my childhood when as a youngster I kept believing my father each time he said he would stop abusing alcohol. Repeated cycles of joy followed by disappointment eventually dampened my ability to express my joy at all. The ability to express my joy is now a focus of my personal development work.
- *You must be stupid* filter—This response filter is the same as the intake filter, only occasionally the words might actually come out of my mouth. I am capable of saying, "You must be stupid." If I want to be obtuse, I can ask questions in such a way as to imply that you must be stupid. I always feel bad after I use this response filter.
- *If you can't say anything nice, don't say anything* filter—This one may be familiar to you. I heard this from adults many times as a child. Unfortunately, those adults did not explain *nice* consistently, so I learned to keep quiet to be on the safe side. As an adult, I have modified this filter and developed my skills so as to be able to say things that might be uncomfortable yet need to be said.
- *Don't comment unless you are positive about what you are saying* filter—This is another filter that kept me quiet a lot. I trapped myself by equating *positive* with *always correct.* Later I learned that I could be *positive* and incorrect and that was okay for most things. It became easier to offer my ideas in brainstorming sessions and other idea-generating situations. Rather than withhold them, I try to qualify my ideas and comments with a measure of certainty (such as percent certain).
- *Always pay my own way* filter—I somehow translated this filter to *don't be a burden on anyone.* If I let someone pay my way for anything, I felt obligated to pay them back as soon as possible. I

kept score on myself. It was okay with me if I paid someone else's way, but the other way around was not acceptable. This prevented me from accepting genuine acts of generosity from others until one day I realized how I was robbing others of the good feelings that come with being generous. Now I don't make much of a fuss when someone wants to buy me dinner or give me a gift. The filter is still active, but not automatic. I can consider each situation in real time and decide how to respond. A filter like this may get in the way of individuals helping each other on a project team. For example, someone may be falling behind on his deliverables, but not ask for help out of fear that he will burden others or that he may be perceived as not carrying his share of the load.

TROPHIES AND TROUBLES

Some filters act like protective devices. They can keep us from being flooded with data. They can enable us to avoid uncomfortable situations. They can enable us to deal quickly with people. In this way, filters are like habits. Habits enable us to act automatically without thinking. When our filters act automatically out of our awareness, we risk losing potentially rich learning experiences. I am not suggesting that you get rid of your filters. Rather, I am suggesting that you become more aware of your filters so that you can choose when and how you use them.

Some filters that protected me when I was 4 years old may not be appropriate now that I am 53. Unfortunately, most filters don't have automatic expiration dates. For example, I now know that not every apparently loud, aggressive person intends to harm me. I have discovered some wonderful people I might previously have written off as a result of my *loud aggressive people* filter.

IDENTIFYING YOUR FILTERS

The first step toward identifying your filters is awareness. Practice becoming aware of when your filters are working. One way to practice is to notice when you are reacting to someone in a way that seems out of proportion to what is happening. Often a strong reaction can be related to one of your intake filters. Try to notice when your internal response—what you would like to do or say to the other person—is different from your external response—what you actually do or say to the other person. The difference, if there is one, might indicate that a response filter is at work.

Keep a journal. Record in your journal each time you have an awareness of one of your filters at work. Try to put words to your filters (as

I have done with mine). Play around with the words. You will know when you have them just right. Some people know by their intuition. Some know by how their body feels. Others know in their hearts. Still others know in their heads. You may also want to ask a good friend to tell you when you are using a filter. Your friend may need a little help from you to know what to look and listen for.

Forgive yourself in advance for not having perfect awareness of all your filters. The awareness takes time and effort. In the beginning, the best you may be able to do is notice after the fact that you have used a filter. With practice, you may be able to notice your filter while it is working. Eventually you may be able to identify a number of your filters. In 13 years, I have discovered 49 of my filters.

USING YOUR AWARENESS TO CHANGE HOW YOU RESPOND

Remember, "difficult" is an interpretation you make. My response to a person with whom I have difficulty is often triggered by the interpretation I make of the that person's behavior and my feelings about that interpretation. One way to change how I respond is to hold off my interpretation until I get more data. My feelings often change when I change my interpretation. This can lead to my having a different response.

For example, let's say that I am a project leader and Mike is a designer on my project. I am having difficulty with Mike because I was expecting his design changes to be finished today per his status report, and they are not. One scenario could have me using my *do what you say you will do* filter to write him off as unreliable. My response in this scenario could be something like, "Mike, I guess I can't rely on you." This puts the blame and the responsibility for my difficulty all on Mike. This kind of response may also cut off communication between Mike and me. It certainly does not invite communication.

In another scenario I might say, "Mike, I thought I read in your status report that you would finish the design changes by today. The changes do not seem to be finished. I'm not sure how to interpret that. What am I missing?" Here, I am giving Mike the benefit of some of my intake and asking him for more data. I am holding off on my interpretation until I hear more from him, and providing him an opportunity to give me more information. Using my *generous interpretation* filter, there might be a perfectly reasonable explanation. This way of responding allows me to be responsible for my difficulty, avoid blaming Mike, and keep the communication going. Instead of labeling Mike a difficult person, I take responsibility for my difficulty with Mike.

To recap:

- When you label someone a difficult person, it is easy to project most, if not all, the responsibility for the difficulty onto that person. When you do that, you give up some of the power you need to deal effectively with him or her.
- Remember that "difficult" is an interpretation *you* make. Intake is not inherently difficult. It is merely words, sounds, and expressions. Our interpretation of the intake is what makes it difficult or not.
- We all have filters. Our filters may be completely out of our awareness or not.
- The first step toward identifying your filters is awareness.
- One way to change how I respond is to hold off my interpretation until I get more data. My feelings often change when I change my interpretation. This can lead to my having a different response.

Try this:

- Complete the following statements in as many ways as you can. "I get really annoyed by someone who…!" or "I hate it when someone…!" Write your answers on paper, perhaps in your journal. Study what you have written. Your answers may help you start identifying your intake filters.
- Sometimes we do not say or do what we would like to say or do. Instead we say or do something else that we think is more acceptable. Try to recall times when you edited your comments this way. Write down as many details as you can remember about what was happening and why you said what you said instead of what you wanted to say. Study your answers. They may help you start to discover some of your response filters.

Chapter 4

HOW DO YOU LIKE LEARNING ABOUT YOURSELF?

As a professional, you probably keep yourself current with your profession's body of knowledge, tools, and methods. If you do not, you may lose some of your effectiveness, not to mention your marketability. Project management professionals can attend certification programs that teach them about managing projects. The focus of such learning tends to be about things—which are outside of you. For example, you can learn about planning and estimating tools and techniques. You can learn about lifecycle models. Let's not forget configuration management and subcontractor management. These are all useful things to know.

Powerful project leadership requires a different kind of learning. Powerful project leadership begins with you. You will need to learn all you can about yourself so that you can develop your ability to lead yourself. The better you are at leading yourself, the more effective you will be at leading your projects out of messy—and inevitable—human system problems. Some of the kinds of problems people get into when they try to work together are personality conflicts, who gets to tell whom what to do, miscommunications, political games, differences in work ethic, skill gaps, and puffed-up egos. Some appear to us as inadvertent and others as just plain mean-spirited. I do not believe such labels are helpful because:

- I cannot see what is inside another person's heart and mind at any given moment.
- I may not see what is in my own heart and mind at any given moment.
- I can give a generous interpretation or a stingy one, but I cannot know with certainty that someone's behavior is inadvertent or mean-spirited.

If you have been alive for more than 15 minutes, chances are you have been a participant in one or more messy human system problems. The key to resolving these kinds of problems lies in your willingness to become aware of and "own" your ways of:

- Taking responsibility
- Trusting and connecting with others
- Handling differentness
- Taking care of yourself
- Handling your upset
- Having your tears.

These are universal human experiences, although the expression of them is unique to each individual. As I become more aware and accepting of my own humanness—by learning about myself—I am better able to understand and appreciate the humanness in others. As I accept my own humanness and that of others, it is easier to connect with them when I choose to. The aim of this chapter is to help you prepare yourself to do this kind of introspective learning about yourself.

READINESS FOR LEARNING

Some of my most powerful learning has come during teachable moments. A teachable moment is a moment when some part of me is ready to receive the lesson. That part may be my brain, my intuition, my skin, my heart, or a combination of parts. Sometimes I get ready by design: I go into the situation with the intention and purpose to learn. I develop my readiness gradually, with a great deal of safety and support. An example might be through personal growth counseling or an experiential workshop where I am working on deep personal issues. I do not always know what the lesson will be, and it may not be enjoyable, but at least it is invited.

Sometimes I am not aware of my readiness at all, like when I get caught being myself. The lesson arrives uninvited, with a sudden and unexpected jolt. This can happen anywhere, at any time. The lesson can come from my wife, my son, a colleague, a business partner, a student, a fellow workshop participant, or a complete stranger.

I have had powerful invited lessons and powerful uninvited lessons. What makes them powerful is how I accept and make sense of them—not whether they are invited.

The best teachers of adults I know have the ability to create learning environments where teachable moments are plentiful. They recognize teachable moments when they occur and offer the lesson to the student with great care. I consider it a gift when these teachers help me catch myself being myself.

For example, my teacher might notice me struggling during an experiential group exercise to get others to listen to my idea. As the group discusses what we learned post-simulation, the teacher might make his observation known to me and ask, "Does this ever happen back at work?" I might have an immediate flash of recognition that, of course, it happens all the time. Maybe for the first time in my life, I become aware that my inability to get others to listen to me is a pattern—in my work life and perhaps even in my personal life. My teacher might then ask, "Would you like some feedback from anyone here about how you could be more successful at getting others to listen to you?" When it is put this way, I have the choice and the opportunity to learn something that could literally change my life.

LEVELS OF LEARNING

I think I learn in levels. Perhaps you do also. You have probably heard the observation that we keep repeating the same lessons until we learn them. I would modify this statement slightly: We keep repeating the same lessons so we can learn them in deeper ways.

Most of us probably do not spend a lot time thinking about how we learn. We just do it. Personally, I believe I developed my ability to *observe what is happening* in five levels:

Level 1: Not observing
Level 2: Observing in the moment; my only job is to observe one or two things
Level 3: Observing in the moment; my only job is to observe six or more things
Level 4: Observing in the moment while participating in the activity I am observing
Level 5: Observing all the time.

I sometimes iterate each level several times before moving to the next level. I may also regress a level after unsuccessfully attempting a move to a higher level. For example, having iterated level 2 several times, I may attempt level 3. If this attempt is unsuccessful, I may go back to level 2 for a few iterations to reset my sense of competence before attempting level 3 again. Opportunities to practice facilitate moving to deeper levels of learning safely—that is, with support and encouragement and without punishment or judgment for less than perfect results.

To illustrate, I'll use the same context for each level. The context is a five-person team attempting to solve a physical puzzle for 10 minutes.

The puzzle contains eight square pieces of wood with a colored dot on each corner of each piece. The pieces must be manipulated by hand to form a specified pattern of matching colored dots.

Level 1: Not observing

I do not intentionally observe anything while it is happening. I just happen to be there. After the fact, if I am asked, I may be able to recall what I saw, heard, smelled, tasted, or touched. I can compare that with sensory data of others who were there to validate the accuracy of my memory. A lot happens that I do not notice.

Level 2: Observing in the moment, but not being involved in solving the puzzle

I intentionally observe what is happening while it is happening. I am in the role of observer. I am not solving the puzzle. My only job is to observe one or two specific things. For example, my job might be to: (1) count how many times each person speaks, and (2) count how many times each person is addressed by his or her name.

With practice, I become pretty good at observing just two things. That information could be useful to the five-person team trying to solve the puzzle. For example, conflicts might surface around someone monopolizing the team's air time or because people cannot tell to whom questions or comments are addressed. A lot still happens that I do not notice.

Level 3: Observing in the moment, and still not being involved in puzzle-solving

I intentionally observe what is happening while it is happening. I am in the role of observer. I am not solving the puzzle. My only job is to observe, although my list of what to observe is growing. For example, my job might be to:

- Count how many times each person speaks.
- Count how many times each person is addressed by his or her name.
- Count how many times each person touches the puzzle pieces.
- Track what happens to an idea after it is spoken.
- Notice where people look when they speak.
- Notice who (if anyone) keeps track of time.

With practice, I become pretty good at tracking several things. I can provide more information to the team that might help them work better together to solve the puzzle. Still, a lot happens that I do not notice.

Level 4: Observing in the moment while being involved in solving the puzzle

I intentionally observe what is happening while it is happening. I am also one of the five people solving the puzzle. My job is to: (1) help my team solve the puzzle in 10 minutes, and (2) observe my team's puzzle-solving process.

This kind of observation is even more difficult. I try to pay attention to the content: solving the puzzle. At the same time, I try to pay attention to the process: how my team is solving the puzzle. If I can do both, the result can be extremely valuable to my team. My feedback can be used in real time to improve our team puzzle-solving process on the fly. With lots of practice, I can become pretty good at this kind of observation, although there will always be things I miss.

Level 5: Observing all the time

When you reach this level of observation skill, you observe all the time because you are convinced that the information will be useful. You may not be sure when or how or to whom it will be useful. You find yourself observing in all kinds of social structures: puzzle-solving sessions, project meetings, meetings with clients, traveling on an airplane, eating in restaurants, relaxing with family or friends, going to the movies, and attending conferences. You find it difficult to turn off your observation skills. You are incredibly useful in all kinds of settings because you notice "everything"—at least that is what people tell you. Of course, you know that a lot of things escape your notice, but that is your little secret. If you get really good at this, you can eventually catch yourself being yourself. As I did with the help of my teacher, you may start to notice your own teachable moments and become aware of your own patterns.

Here is another example: changing a specific behavior. For this example, I will use raising my voice as the behavior. I have observed this behavior so many times in project settings that I would be willing to bet that anyone who has ever worked on a project has had to deal with this behavior. Of course, I was oblivious to raising my own voice. My partner told me about this behavior. At first I did not believe her. Now I know that I do raise my voice, and I know some of the reasons why. Sometimes when I feel unsure of myself, I raise my voice. I suppose I do that to sound more convincing. I sometimes raise my voice when I am asked to repeat what I have said. I suppose I do that so she will hear me better. Here are the levels I recall going through to learn about raising my voice.

Level 1: Completely oblivious

I do not know I am raising my voice. Therefore, it does not occur to me to ask for feedback about the behavior. I'm totally unaware of the effect that raising my voice has on other people. If someone gives me unsolicited feedback about it, I become defensive and blow it off.

Level 2: Somewhat oblivious

I am unaware that I am raising my voice. I may start to suspect this behavior after repeated unsolicited feedback. I am open to feedback, perhaps from a specific person I trust, like my partner. I care about the effect that raising my voice has on her. I still may want to blow it off, but her feedback means a lot to me. She has a way of giving me the feedback that is not blaming or judgmental.

Level 3: Recognizing the behavior after the fact

I accept that I raise my voice sometimes. I want to increase my awareness of when I do it. I want my voice-raising to be a choice, not an automatic, knee-jerk response. With some practice, I can now recognize when I have done it, but only immediately afterward. "Yikes! I did it again!"

Level 4: Recognizing the behavior in the moment

With lots more practice and awareness, I begin to recognize when I am raising my voice as it happens. I may say to myself, "Look at that. I am raising my voice." Then I can choose to do something different or not. I may still raise my voice, for instance, so the other person can hear me over some competing noise. The difference is that raising my voice is a matter of choice, not an automatic response out of my awareness.

Level 5: Predicting the behavior before it happens based on many cycles

After many cycles of catching myself raising my voice in the moment, I can see patterns emerging. For example, I now know that I am more likely to raise my voice when:

- I am overtired.
- I am not feeling well.
- I am questioning my own competence or value.

So when I can be aware that I am overtired, not feeling well, or questioning my own competence, I can be extra vigilant about my voice.

Here is a third example: learning to fish.

Level 1: Imitating others

When I first started fishing as a young boy, I watched how others did it and tried to imitate them. My observation skills were not as honed as they are now so I failed to notice many finer details. For example, with my young eyes I saw casting as largely an arm movement. I did not appreciate the physics of the rod nor the contribution of my wrist movement to accurate casting. In fact, I was not concerned with accuracy at all, feeling good if I managed to cast the bait or lure into the water instead of a tree or myself. When I managed to catch a fish, it was a complete mystery to me how I did it. I just considered myself lucky.

Level 2: Proper tackle and proper use

I began to learn the differences between types of tackle. Bait casting gear, spin casting gear, and fly casting gear are different and are used differently in various kinds of water and terrain. Fishing line can be braided or monofilament and can have different weight-tested limits. Rods and fishing lines can be matched for optimum casting and fish-handling ability. Artificial baits come in different sizes and weights and can be matched to rods and fishing lines. Having the right gear for the water and terrain and type of fish seemed to result in my catching more fish. But it was still a mystery to me why I caught fish.

Level 3: Casting, landing techniques, and developing a feel for the strike

Now I am learning more casting techniques. Each technique is appropriate for placing my lure or fly precisely where I want it in specific situations. For example, a barrel or hoop cast will work when there is too much brush or tree cover behind me to use a conventional fly casting technique. Of course, hooking a fish is not enough. I have to land the fish, meaning get it into my hands so I can keep it for eating or release it back into the water. I learn to take my time and not try to overpower the fish. Let it run and fight and tire itself. Then I can either net the fish with a hand-held net or land it with a hand technique such as grasping the lower jaw to lift it out of the water.

Although I am getting better at hooking and landing fish, it is still pretty much a mystery how the fish ends up on my hook. I am getting a lot of strikes but not hooking the fish. It seems I am just a little too late or a little too early in setting the hook. Eventually, I learn how to watch my line and, with my finger on the line, develop a feel for the strike. Each kind of fish has a different strike pattern. Some practically hook themselves as they literally attack the lure. Others are more cautious and subtle when they strike. When dry fly fishing, I learn to keep my eye on the fly as it floats by. This not easy because some flies are very tiny.

Hooking fish is less of a mystery now. I am hooking and landing more fish per strike. For example, if I get 50 strikes in a day of fishing, I can hook and land 25 or more fish.

Level 4: Learning about cover, temperature, spawning, food, genetic response

At this level, I am reading articles and books and watching the fishing programs on TV. I am learning about the kind of underwater cover game fish like: weed beds, rocky points, shelves, troughs, and trees. I learn that water temperature matters. Game fish do not always stay in one spot. They move depending on water temperature, water turbidity, and food sources. Some lure manufacturers claim they have studied genetic response: why certain fish strike a lure and why not. Apparently there are reasons other than hunger—such as defending territory and fight-or-flight response.

Now I am catching fish consistently in certain places with which I am familiar. Most of the mystery is gone now. I am a little sad about that.

Level 5: Catching fish consistently anywhere

Now I am traveling to different waters all over the United States. I am fishing in world-class bass lakes and trout rivers. A quick check with a local guide service is usually all I need to discover which lures and flies are hot, what the current hatch is, and where in the water fish are holding. A hatch refers to the kind of insect that has just come out of the chrysalis stage and is flying just over the water's surface. Fish eat these insects as they fall on the water. I try to match my fly to the insect. I discover all this information as I am purchasing my fishing permit and gear: lures, flies, line, and other essentials. I release nearly all the fish I catch unharmed back into the water. Many of my trout flies are made with barbless hooks to make the release even easier.

At this level, I simply enjoy being in communion with nature. Fishermen at this level seem to find each other easily. We enjoy sharing these moments on pristine waters with each other. The places I fish are so beautiful and spiritual that I really do not care if I catch fish at all. I love the thrill of hooking a fish, but that is no longer the main course. It is dessert.

There is nothing magic about the number of levels. It is merely coincidence that the preceding three examples have five levels. You may discover that you learn some things in four levels and others in five or six levels.

THE VALUE OF A LEARNING PARTNER

How much of what others can see of you can you see? Look at yourself without the aid of a mirror. What can you see—shoulders, chest, belly, part of your arms, hands, front of thighs, knee caps, tops of your feet? There is a lot of you that you can't see. We are not designed to be able to see ourselves very well. Virginia Satir said, " We need an extra arm with eyes to see ourselves."[1] Our physical design limits our ability to learn about ourselves. We need feedback. We need to know how we look to others, how we come across. A learning partner can help us see ourselves and give us feedback.

Learning about yourself can be scary because you may need to reveal some of your vulnerability. Your learning partner needs to be someone who:

- You can trust with your vulnerability
- Will tell you their truth about what they see and hear
- Will not try to protect you from the truth, and not judge you
- Understands how difficult this kind of learning is
- Wants the same kind of learning support from you.

A learning partner can give you valuable feedback about your facial expressions, voice, mannerisms, and body language. For example, you might not be able to notice the light in your eyes. Your learning partner might ask you, "Did you know that your eyes really sparkle and light up when you talk?" A learning partner can help you catch yourself being yourself, such as my partner letting me know when I am raising my voice. Or perhaps your partner will let you know that your intentions are difficult to determine from your actions. A learning partner cannot see inside your heart and mind, but can ask you questions about what you are feeling and thinking. Your learning partner can tell you how you look on the outside and together you can explore how that matches what you are thinking and feeling.

[1]Seminar, Family: Impact in Relationships, Workplace, and Community, St. Louis, MO, April 16-17, 1986.

To recap:

- Learning all you can about yourself is essential to powerful project leadership.
- Readiness for learning about yourself is about how you open yourself to teachable moments. You can plan and prepare yourself for some teachable moments in whatever ways fit for you. Other teachable moments arrive uninvited.
- Learning about yourself sometimes occurs in levels. Each level builds on the previous level. Opportunities to practice safely facilitate deeper levels of learning.
- A learning partner can help you see yourself in ways you cannot because of the way our bodies are designed. Your learning partner can help you catch yourself being yourself.

Try this:

"Meta learning" means learning about learning. Two topics discussed in this chapter are meta learning topics: (1) readiness for learning about yourself, and (2) levels of learning. Here are some other ideas for learning about yourself. If possible, check your answers with someone you trust who knows you well.

1. How do you handle receiving bad news?
2. How do you handle giving bad news?
3. How do you handle not being able to make good on a commitment?
4. How do you handle conflict between two people who report to you?
5. When is it most difficult for you to make a decision?
6. When is it most difficult for you to say "no" to your boss?
7. How do you handle a very public success?
8. How do you handle a very public failure?
9. What have been some of your most memorable lessons, and how did those arrive?
10. Describe the levels of progression to reach your current proficiency at something you really enjoy doing, such as a sport or hobby.

Chapter 5
BEING UNDERSTOOD

"Pay attention to what I mean, not what I say," my father would sometimes say to me when I was a kid. I did not know what to make of that. To me it appeared that sometimes he said what he meant, and sometimes he did not. My problem was that I couldn't tell which was which. On a good day I could get it right about half the time. On a bad day I could not get it right at all. As a youngster I was confused and frustrated by my apparent inability to understand what my father wanted. I was equally frustrated that I could not seem to make myself understood. Although we never talked about it, my father probably did not feel understood by me either. As a result, we were not very good together. By that I mean he and I could not effectively do the work of creating the family we wanted to be, and although we enjoyed many happy moments together, he and I missed out on a lot of potentially satisfying experiences with each other.

What does my story have to do with powerful project leadership? The work of your project team is to create something of value together. The created value lies not just in the product or service being built and delivered. There is also value in growing your team's capability to work together effectively to build and deliver the next product, and the next, and so on. There are lots of aspects to "work together effectively." Some typical ones are roles, responsibilities, decision-making, problem-solving, conflict resolution, clear lines of authority, assigning and tracking work, and communication. All these are facilitated by understanding one another. When you and your team members feel understood by each other, the team is better able to do its work of creating such value. When you and your team members are not good together, you may have great difficulty creating the value you seek.

A powerful project leader continually works hard at being understood and at understanding others. In doing so, she provides a model for the rest of the team to emulate.

TWO WAYS OF BEING UNDERSTOOD

We all want our words, our message, what we are trying to say to others, to be understood. In our communication, we want others to understand the message we intend. Life just seems to go easier when we are understood in this way. Our communication is straight. There are fewer misunderstandings to clear up. People find it easier to trust our message. All kinds of relationships, both professional and personal, generally work better. For example, when someone disagrees with me, it is easier for me to handle when I know that my message is understood. If I do not know whether or not my message is understood, then I am uncertain whether the person disagrees with my intended message or the misunderstood one.

Understanding does not automatically mean agreement or acceptance. Although I may hope for agreement, I do not expect that anyone will always agree with my message. I do, however, want my message to be understood.

I think we each want to be understood in another way—for who we are. For example, I want some people (but not necessarily everyone) to understand *me*. I mean the *me* who wants to be loved and accepted completely—with all my good parts and ugly parts. Paradoxically, for others to understand me in this way, I have to risk letting them know me more than just superficially. That can be risky. What people know about me can be used to help or to hurt me. When the risk feels too great, I can protect myself by keeping others at a distance emotionally. I may let them see only the parts of me that I think are acceptable and valued.

For example, if I think others accept and value being strong, I may show them my strength. I may not show them my weakness for fear that they may not accept and value me. My belief that I have to be strong all the time around others can be a huge burden that wears me out. While I may accept this burden because it feels less risky to me than doing otherwise, it also hinders my being understood in a deeper way. Sometimes when I feel weak, I would really like to show it on the outside and know that I am still valued. Fortunately, the choice—understand me completely or not at all—does not have to be binary. I can choose to reveal myself gradually over time, first to myself, then to one other person, and then to more when I feel safe enough.

Having our messages understood and having ourselves understood are universal struggles. In this chapter, I will focus on our messages being understood. I will not explore the struggle of having ourselves understood. I mention it here briefly because I have seen how one sometimes affects the other. I have seen evidence of this in my consulting work with troubled projects. For example, I find that often many people on a troubled project know that the project is headed for trouble long before the trouble is officially acknowledged by management (if it ever is). When asked how it happened that problems so many people knew about went unaddressed for so long, their explanations usually fall into one of three patterns:

Pattern 1: "My message of concern was not understood, so I guess I am not a good communicator—or I do not deserve to be heard, or there is something lacking in me." These individuals interpreted that their messages were not understood as a weakness or flaw in themselves. They tried to tell somebody their message of concern, but there was no evidence that their message was understood. Some kept trying for awhile and then gave up.

Pattern 2: "I was sure I would be misunderstood, so I never communicated my message." These individuals perceived themselves as incapable of being understood correctly, so they assumed their message would be misunderstood. They did not tell anybody their message of concern, fearing that they would be labeled naysayers, or because they noticed others trying and saw that it did no good or that the intentions of those speaking up were questioned or misjudged.

Pattern 3: Occasionally, a small number of individuals never stopped trying to communicate their message of concern about the project. These individuals viewed their unheeded messages as information about the receivers of their messages. They did not seem to interpret this as a negative reflection on their message or themselves.

FIVE LEVELS OF COMMUNICATION

We reveal our messages and ourselves through our communication. According to Dr. Gary Chapman's model,[1] we all communicate on five levels.

Cliché

The cliché level of communication is the most superficial and least revealing of the deeper me, that is, the me that I want others to understand but at the same time fear them understanding. This level of communication is sometimes referred to as chit-chat, small talk, plati-

[1]Gary Chapman and Betty Hassler, *Communication and Intimacy* (Nashville: LifeWay Press, 1992), p. 20.

tudes, or breaking the ice. One benefit of clichés is that they permit us to appear sociable without intruding or invading someone's personal space. Another is that clichés are safe. Neither person has to reveal much, and the emotional energy required in this kind of communication is minimal.

However, the benefits that clichés confer can also be their drawbacks when they are overused or used inappropriately. Friends, family, associates, co-workers, and partners usually expect more intimacy. If communication is always clichéd, it is nearly impossible to achieve the sort of intimacy that deeper relationships thrive on. Examples of clichéd communication might include comments or questions and responses such as:

"Nice day, huh?" "Beautiful!"
"How about those Yankees?" "Yes, they're terrific."
"How's your project going?" "Fine. How 'bout yours?"
"Boy, this elevator is slow." "Yeah, like molasses in January."
"Come here often?" "Oh, occasionally."
"Traveling on business or pleasure?" "Business."

Information

When we communicate on this level of giving information, we convey a message that is more substantial than platitudes. We can give information without revealing too much of ourselves. For example, I can report a decision that was made in a project meeting, I can give you directions to my house, hours of operation, basketball scores, lunch menu in the cafeteria. . . . We can filter information, giving only the information we feel safe giving. For example, my response to, "How's your project going?" from my wife might include more information than I would provide in response to the same question from a peer or a boss. I might tell my wife some of the less pleasant aspects of the project, while I might tell a peer about only the good things that are happening.

Opinions

When we communicate at this level, giving opinions, we start to reveal more of ourselves. My opinions are personal. They are a part of me. I own them. If I share my opinion, I risk someone knowing something about me. This is different from giving information about things outside me. When I give my opinion, I am talking about me. Someone may not like my opinion. He may hold it against me or try to punish me. He may even judge me, not just my opinion.

For example, say you are a team lead attending a project management meeting, and the executive sponsor, without warning, asks you,

"What is your opinion of the new estimates to complete for this project?" It may feel risky to give your opinion in the presence of your peer team leads, project manager, and executive sponsor.

Feelings

Communicating feelings is the next level of communication. Feelings are very personal, perhaps even more so than opinions. Feelings describe our emotional state. The language of feelings is something that must be developed. In the workplace, the safe expression of strong feelings is still somewhat of an enigma, mostly because we have not learned how to deal appropriately with strong feelings—either our own or others. For example, if Karen (whom you barely know) cordially asks you, "How are you?" and you reply, "I feel lousy and depressed," this could be more than Karen ever wanted to know about you. It is important to consider how your expression of feelings might affect others.

Total Truth

The fifth level of communicating is telling the total truth. Total truth is that stuff inside you that you cannot bring yourself to communicate to anyone but a very small number of people, perhaps a therapist or a religious leader. It might be a deep dark secret, or it might be something wonderful that you have not known how to express. You may not communicate for fear that the truth might hurt someone or drive them away from you. There was a time when I would not speak my total truth to anyone, not one person, not even myself. I do now, but I reserve total truth for only a very few people.

Telling someone your total truth is the most emotionally intimate thing you will ever do. It requires careful consideration of context and of the effects it might have on the person you are telling. For example, when you are in a hurry and rushing out the door is probably not a good time to speak your total truth.

When I finally took the risk, it felt like what I imagine jumping off the south rim of the Grand Canyon without a parachute would feel like—only I didn't die. It was an amazing threshold to cross. My whole life changed. It changed the way I see myself and how I relate to others. To tell my truth, and still be loved and accepted, helped me be more loving and accepting of others. I can now appreciate the fear and sense of risk involved in crossing that threshold.

Here is an example of the profound effect that total truth can have.

During a project review, I was interviewing one of the executive sponsors of the project. I started simply by asking him to tell me about the project. He started ranting and raving about how his project director had made a mess of things. His face got red and his voice got loud. He pounded the table. The project involved implementation of a major ERP system, which was years late and millions of dollars overrun. After spending huge amounts of money and time, what they had was barely usable. To add more pressure, the year 2000 was a year away and the sponsor had no confidence that the system would even function on January 1, 2000.

After listening to his rant, I said, "Rich, you seem very angry about all this. Are you?" He said, "Damn right I am angry! I hate it when we do stupid things!" I said calmly, "I wonder. Do you think some of your anger is with yourself—that you feel somewhat responsible for the mess?" Rich got very quiet for a moment. He heaved a big sigh. His body loosened. Then he said in a smaller voice, "Well, yes. I am the one who put the project in the hands of this project director. But what do I know about hiring a project director? I'm a Ph.D. economist, not a techie person." I said, "Thank you for saying that, Rich. I think we are on to something very important now."

I heard later in a roundabout way that two weeks after my interview with Rich, he stood up in an all-hands meeting of project team members and users and said, "I feel somewhat responsible for the mess this project is in, and now see that I have not been a very good executive sponsor. How could I be? I have absolutely no experience being a sponsor for an IT project. I'm an economist for goodness sake, not a techie person. I would like us all to put our energy into getting this project back on track. We now know what went wrong and what we have to do going forward." What seemed so extraordinary about Rich, I was told by people who knew him, was that he did not seem like the kind of executive who would stand up and admit something like that in public.

From that point on, I started to see a shift in the project. With some coaching, Rich became a more involved and active sponsor. I saw less blaming and more creative problem-solving. The project made it back on track in time for January 1, 2000, and later that year the project was declared successful. It took a lot for Rich to say his truth, first to me privately, and then to the project team. It had a profound effect on him and the entire project community.

WHAT KEEPS OUR MESSAGES FROM BEING UNDERSTOOD, AND WHAT CAN WE DO ABOUT IT?

It is a small miracle that any communication is ever understood by anyone when you consider how many things can go wrong with a single interaction. Consider some of the following things that can go wrong, and what you can do to increase the chances of your message being understood.

Receiver Gets Your Words Wrong

When your primary language is a second language to some members of your team, words, phrases, and sentence structure can sometimes be difficult to understand because the receiver is translating as you speak. It gets even more difficult for the receiver when you add slang or jargon, speed up when excited, or try to talk over a lot of noise. Even when everyone speaks the same primary language, the imprecise use of words, not having the receiver's full attention, and the influence of input and response filters can distort your message so that the receiver does not get all your words or gets them incorrectly. (See Chapter 3 for more on filters.)

What to do:

Be as precise with your words as you can. Try to make sure you have the receiver's full attention, and he is not distracted by other people or things. Speak as clearly as you can. Ask the receiver respectfully to repeat key parts of your message to check for accuracy. This is a quality check for both of you, not merely a test to see if the receiver is listening. It is a quality check for you to see if you said what you meant to say. It is a quality check for the receiver to see if he got your message correctly. This quality check may feel a bit awkward at first, but it can avoid some miscommunications.

Receiver Interprets Your Words Incorrectly

Even if the receiver hears all your words correctly, he may incorrectly interpret what your words mean. You can sometimes tell right away when someone does not get your meaning, such as when he responds in a completely surprising way. At other times you may not be able to tell, such as when she leaves nodding in agreement and saying, "Yes, okay," and later you learn that she completely misinterpreted what you intended.

What to do:

One way to minimize your message being misunderstood is to package your intended meaning with your message. You can say something like, "blah, blah, blah, *and by that I mean* bleh, bleh, bleh." For example, at the beginning of this chapter I said, "As a result we were not very good together. By that I mean he and I could not effectively to do the work of creating the family we wanted to be, and although we enjoyed many happy moments together, he and I missed out on a lot of potentially satisfying experiences with each other." Adding the *by that I mean* helps reduce the number of possible interpretations of "As a result we were not very good together." This is not foolproof because the words you use to describe your intended meaning can themselves be misinterpreted.

Receiver Does Not Know How Significant Your Message Is to You

Significance is a measure of how important something is to you. Without significance, we would be overwhelmed with information all the time. Significance allows us to prioritize information so we can deal with the most important first. If your message is important to you, you are likely to have strong feelings about it. It may not be understood as you intend if you fail to communicate the significance. Other people have no way to tell what is significant to us unless we tell them. If the receiver knows how significant your message is to you, his understanding of your message may be more like you hope it will be. Sharing significance is an example of level 4 communication.

What to do:

Tell others the significance, to you, of your message. Use the pronoun "I" with feeling words such as:

- I hope.
- I am worried or concerned.
- I am excited.
- I am disappointed.

Here is an example: Notice the use of "I am hoping" and " I am concerned."

> Dear Jack,
>
> Please scrutinize this draft carefully. I will call you in a few days to set up a time we can discuss your feedback and suggestions.
>
> By scrutinize I mean really examine it in detail. I will be much more confident in the plan with your input. I am hoping you will spot potential risks and opportunities based on your extensive experience with projects of this size and complexity. I am concerned that I may have missed something important.
>
> Thank you in advance for your help.
>
> Alice

HOW TO TELL WHETHER YOUR MESSAGE IS UNDERSTOOD

You know your messages are not understood when you catch yourself frequently saying, "Sorry, that's not what I meant." Other clues that can give you cause to check further for understanding include:

- When you get a reaction you do not expect or that surprises you, such as what seems like an angry response, a puzzled or frustrated facial expression, no visible reaction at all, or simply silence
- When someone does not agree with you and in discussing the disagreement further, you both discover a misunderstanding
- When someone attributes something to you that does not fit, like anger, fear, embarrassment, or some bad intention
- When someone gives the worst possible interpretation to your message.

The best way to tell if your message is understood is first to observe the receiver carefully while you are communicating your message, and then afterward to see if you get the behavior you expect. Of course, you will need to know what to look for. Here are a few things I look for to tell me if my message is understood:

I know my message is understood when the receiver:

- Makes eye contact with me—not staring me down, but giving me enough eye contact that I perceive he is paying attention.
- Periodically repeats my words back to me to verify accuracy.
- Shares his interpretation with me to verify what I meant, or give me an opportunity to clarify my meaning.
- Asks me how important my message, my question, or concern is to me.
- Asks questions to probe for details that I might mistakenly assume are known.
- Disagrees with my message on the basis of his understanding. Probing the disagreement can sometimes reveal whether he understood my message.
- Follows up with behavior I would expect to see. For example, if he understood I wanted a meeting scheduled with him and he agreed he would do it, then I'd know he understood when the meeting was in fact scheduled.

GIVE THE GIFT OF UNDERSTANDING

One excellent way to get more understanding is to give more understanding. All the material in this chapter can, with practice, increase your chances of getting your messages understood. The same material can help you understand the messages of others. For example, consider the various ways you can tell if your message is understood, such as when the receiver makes eye contact, asks you questions, and verifies your meaning. You can use these same techniques to let others know that you understand their message. I encourage you to practice, practice, practice the techniques in this chapter. You will be pleased with the increased quality of your relationships with others.

To recap:

- The work of your project team is to create something of value together.
- When you and your team members feel understood by each other, the team is better able to do its work of creating such value.
- A powerful project leader continually works hard at being understood and at understanding others. In doing so, she provides a model for the rest of the team to emulate.
- There are two ways we want to be understood. We want our words and our message to be understood. We also want to be understood for who we are.
- We reveal our messages and ourselves through our communication. According to Dr. Gary Chapman's model, we all communicate on five levels: cliché, information, opinions, feelings, and total truth.
- The best way to tell if your message is understood is to observe the receiver carefully while you are communicating your message, and afterward to see if you get the behavior you expect. Of course, you will need to know what to look for.
- One excellent way to get more understanding is to give more understanding.

Try this:

The next time you have a conversation with a close friend or associate, each of you try to track the conversation in terms of the five levels of communication. Roughly estimate the percentage of time at each level. Compare notes. How close were your estimates? Discuss with your friend or associate what was easy and what was difficult about knowing when you switched from one level to another.

Chapter 6

WHEN YOU WANT TO RUN AWAY AND HIDE

Being a powerful project leader will not make you immune to errors in judgment, puzzling interactions, bumpy relationships, or the physical and emotional responses that go with them. These things are natural for us all. Sooner or later we all will be confronted with a project situation that will stretch us beyond our capabilities at that moment. The vignettes of Alice, Robert, and Terry from Part One, Leading Yourself, are examples of project leaders who were in such situations. When that happens, it is possible to feel many things, both physical and emotional, as Alice, Robert, and Terry did.

Here are some ways that other project leaders have described how they felt. I have at various times felt each of these myself. See if any ring a bell:

- "It was difficult to breathe."
- "I felt numb."
- "I felt paralyzed. I could not move my feet."
- "My mouth dried up. It was difficult to speak with my tongue stuck to the roof of my mouth."
- "I felt nauseated."
- "I felt threatened."
- "My brain would not work. My voice was fine. I just could not think of anything to say."
- "I was sure my absolute worst self was out there for all the world to see."
- "I felt worthless."
- "I felt incompetent and stupid."
- "I wanted to hit something."
- "I felt a sense of impending doom."

It may not surprise you that anyone feeling such things could want to run away and hide. (I call it "RAaH" for short.) This is not necessarily a bad strategy—at times it is the best any of us can do. I personally take some comfort in knowing that the choice is always available to me. You do not have to physically go anywhere to run away and hide (although you might). You may run away and hide for a short or for a long time. RAaH can be either figurative or literal. We each have our own unique ways of doing it. Here are few ways I've known it to be done:

- Blow up loudly in public.
- Stew quietly in private.
- Take unscheduled vacations alone.
- Become depressed.
- Self-medicate.
- Bury oneself in work.
- Get physically sick.
- Busy oneself with easy, unimportant tasks.
- Play a computer game.

Running away and hiding seems to be a fairly common human response—judging from so many song lyrics and poems that contain the words "run away and hide." The idea is captured humorously in scene eight, "The French Castle/Wooden Rabbit," from the movie *Monty Python and the Holy Grail.*[1] Graham Chapman as King Arthur commands "Run away!" after the Frenchmen begin catapulting large animals over the castle wall at him and his brave knights. In this movie it was what Arthur and his knights did when they did not know what else to do. "Run away! Run away!"

Although it may be human and natural, it is certainly no laughing matter when you find yourself in that situation. RAaH can temporarily take you out of the self, other, and context picture. The length of time you are out of the picture may be seconds or it may be longer—minutes, hours, even days. While you are out of the picture, you likely will not be very effective at leading anyone, including yourself, or helping your project. This is because you can become disconnected from your sense of worth. You can lose awareness of your own power and your ability to use it. It can be very difficult to make respectful and caring contact with others. When you are not in the picture, your senses can be diminished so that you may not be able to see clearly the context you are in.

---

[1]Copyright © 1974 National Film Trustee Company Limited. All rights reserved.

PUT YOURSELF BACK IN THE PICTURE

Should you want to do so, there are some things you can do to put yourself back in the picture. The first step is awareness. Learn to recognize the signals from your body that let you know that the RAaH moment has arrived. For example, I become very quiet, I hold my breath, my face feels flushed and hot, and my ears ring. I look for the nearest exit. I try to find a place where nobody can see me.

When you recognize the familiar signals, the next step is to remember to breathe. This is very important because when you are in the RAaH state you may not be breathing properly. Your brain gets more oxygen and works better when you breathe properly. Use whatever breathing techniques you know, whether from Yoga, Tai Chi, Aikido, breathing meditation, and so on. If you do not know any such techniques, simply inhale as much air as your lungs can comfortably hold. Then exhale all the air you can. Repeat this two or more times until you feel your body relax somewhat (but not so many times that you start to feel dizzy.) You may notice that your awareness and your ability to think increase somewhat.

The next step is to give yourself permission in advance not to do everything perfectly—the steps being described in this chapter—to put yourself back in the picture. If you have a rule about doing things perfectly, you may have to work on transforming the rule before you can do this step. (See Chapter 9 for instructions on how to transform rules into guides.)

Next, remember the following tools and techniques and use them to help you put yourself back in the picture. More details about these tools and techniques can be found in Chapter 1 (The Zeroeth Step), Chapter 2 (Using Your Internal Resources), and Chapter 15 (Substitutes for Time).

The Zeroeth Step

The zeroeth step is a technique designed to help you focus on important questions before you officially kick off your project—before the inevitable pressure sets in. But you can use the zeroeth step in any situation for which you need self-awareness, balance, and self-direction. The zeroeth step involves taking time just for you. It is like a health spa for your mind and spirit. It can give you the edge you need to keep yourself in the picture and do your best. Use the following modified questions about self:

- Am I breathing properly?
- How am I taking myself out of the picture now?

- What feelings are surfacing for me now as I think about my current situation?
- What tools, resources, and strengths do I have that could help me now?
- What kind of support do I need to put myself back in the picture?
- Who could give me that support?

Your Internal Resources

Remember the following internal resources that you were born with. Use the appropriate ones to help you reconnect with your worth and get your power back.

Thoughts. Use your ability to have your thoughts and think for yourself to get some of your power back. You can *think what you really think instead what you should think*. When you do not fully use your thinking resource, such as when you allow others to tell you what to think, you limit yourself. You give away some of your power.

Feelings. Use your ability to *feel what you feel instead of what you should feel*. Be honest with yourself about what you are feeling even though you may struggle to find the words. Again, some people may try to tell you what to feel. When you do not acknowledge or use your feelings, it is like giving away some of your power. When you claim your feelings, you get some power back.

Wants. Use your ability to *ask for what you want instead of always waiting for permission*. This does not mean that you will get what you ask for. But, you increase your chances if you ask. Waiting for permission usually does not work so well because it requires the permission-giver to be able to read your mind.

Voice. Use your ability to *say what you really see, hear, think, and feel instead of what you ought to say*. Your voice includes all forms of expressing yourself, whether it is speaking, signing, writing, singing, painting, or other mediums. You can act more powerfully when you claim your voice. Choose your moments wisely, however, because there are still places in the world where expressing what you really think and feel can be dangerous to your health.

Risk-taking. Use your ability to *take risks in your own behalf instead of choosing to be only secure and not rock the boat*. You can go for something you want to try even though it may not work out the way you imagined.

Self-Esteem Maintenance Kit

Remember the birth tools from the self esteem maintenance kit. Use them as physical reminders of your ability to access your internal resources and act powerfully in your own behalf.

Wishing Wand. The wishing wand represents your ability to have and to articulate your wishes and hopes. Your wishes and hopes often are a source of motivation. You can touch the wishing wand to remind you of your power to articulate your wishes and hopes.

Courage Stick. The courage stick represents your ability to activate your courage. Your courage empowers you to take action even when you know there will be difficulties. Sometimes you may need your courage to take a first little step like:

- Take a couple of deep breaths
- Ask for the time you need to collect yourself
- Ask a difficult question
- Stand when sitting
- Sit when standing.

You can touch the courage stick as a physical reminder of your courage to go for something you really want—or to say no to something that does not fit.

Wisdom Box. The wisdom box represents your ability to connect with your deepest knowing about what fits for you. Your wisdom box might be that small, still voice inside you that tries to give you direction. Virginia Satir believed that our wisdom box connects us to the wisdom of the universe. You can touch the wisdom box to remind you to access your wisdom.

Golden Key. The golden key represents your ability to open any door and check out new possibilities. Use your golden key to follow your curiosity into the unknown.

Detective Hat. The detective hat represents your ability to investigate and explore without judging. Use your detective hat whenever there is a puzzle, or a question, or an effort to understand. The detective hat empowers you to ask the unaskable and speak the unspeakable in your search for truth.

Yes/No Medallion. The yes/no medallion represents your ability to choose with integrity. On one side the medallion says "yes." On the other side it says "no." Both are respectful, caring words. Your real yes carries with it your awareness and conscious choice to say, "Thank you for asking. Yes. What you ask fits for me at this time." Your real no carries with it your awareness and conscious choice to say, "Thank you for asking. No. What you ask does not fit for me at this time." Use your medallion to keep you strong in your integrity by saying your real yes and your real no.

Heart. The heart represents your ability to have and share your feelings. Feelings are information for you about what is happening inside yourself. Your feelings are what enable you to make a heart connection with another person, should you choose to do that. By heart connection, I mean a mutual sharing of something significant at the feeling level, such as joy or sadness. Use the heart to put you in touch with your feelings.

Substitutes for Time

If the time pressure tyrant is contributing to your RAaH, remember these three things:

1. It only seems like the pressure is coming from the outside. In actuality, you may be pressuring yourself. You could be your own time pressure tyrant!
2. You can reframe time. Changing the frame can change how you see time, much like changing the frame on a picture changes how you see the picture.
3. It is possible to get more time from your time by using "substitutes for time," paradoxical as that may seem. These substitutes are ways to enhance our use of time or change our experience of time.

Here are some substitutes for time that you can read more about in Chapter 15:

- Trust
- Focus
- Asking for help
- Clear communication
- Clear decision-making
- Clear roles and responsibilities
- Clear thinking
- Courage
- Delegating
- Documentation

- Exercise
- Health
- Observing
- Planning
- Priorities
- A repeatable process
- Reuse
- The right number of staff
- Sleep
- Support
- Teamwork
- The right tools.

The point of putting yourself back in the picture is to remind you of and reconnect you with your own power and internal resources. When you are connected to your power, you are better able to make respectful and caring contact with others. You can better see the context you are in. You once again have your most powerful resource—your ability to lead yourself.

BE PREPARED FOR THE NEXT TIME

My partner has her own RAaH emergency kit, which she keeps in a black backpack. You may want to consider creating one for yourself. You can be as creative as you like with your RAaH emergency kit. Find a container such as a backpack, briefcase, computer case, duffel bag, lunch box, tool case, tote bag, overnight bag, or something else that will hold all your emergency gear. You may want to keep it small so that you can transport it easily or carry it with you.

Your survival gear may include objects that remind you of what you need when you feel like you want to run away and hide. What helps you? For example, my partner has an oxygen mask to remind her to breathe. I have a Swiss army knife to remind me of my "MacGyver"[2] part (the part of me who can solve any problem quickly with a piece of wire and basic chemistry or physics). Some other possibilities include:

- A signed permission slip reminding you that you have permission not to do everything perfectly—your signature of course.
- A certificate of temporary incompetence. This can be a useful item for learning new things. The certificate is your assurance that the incompetence is only temporary.

[2]Reference to MacGyver courtesy of Paramount Pictures.

- A stuffed critter or two that have special significance to remind you that you are loveable, or strong, or wise, or for whatever you need reminding.
- Your own partial or complete self-esteem maintenance kit with objects such as the wishing wand, courage stick, wisdom box, golden key, detective hat, yes/no medallion, and heart.
- A substitutes-for-time card deck (see Chapter 15) to remind you of how to get more time from your time.
- A St. Jude prayer card. (St. Jude is the patron saint of hopeless causes!)
- A list of difficult projects or tasks that you have successfully accomplished.

To recap:

- Being a powerful project leader will not make you immune to errors in judgment, puzzling interactions, bumpy relationships, or the physical and emotional responses that go with them.
- Wanting to run away and hide is one possible reaction to being stretched beyond our capabilities at a particular moment in time.
- When we actually do run away and hide—RAaH for short—we each do it our own way. RAaH is not necessarily a bad strategy. Sometimes it is the best any of us can do in that moment.
- When you run away and hide, this can temporarily take you out of the self, other, and context picture.
- There are things you can do to put yourself back in the picture. Breathing is one of the most important. There are also specific tools and techniques that can help you put yourself back in the picture.

Try this:

1. Journal your RAaH experiences. Write down in your journal what is happening at the moment, what feelings you are aware of, what might have triggered your RAaH, and what you have tried or intend to try to put yourself back in the picture. Capturing this information over time can help you get clearer on how it happens, and what works best to put you back in the picture.
2. Start your own RAaH emergency kit by choosing only one object that will remind you of something important you need to do to put yourself back in the picture. Keep the object on your desk in a place that is visible to you.

Part Two
LEADING OTHERS

Leading others is not a substitute for project management. When you are in charge of projects, you need to apply sound project management practices. By practices, I mean planning, organizing, integrating, measuring, and revising activities such as those described by Meilir Page-Jones in his book, *Practical Project Management.*[1] Richard Bechtold describes planning, tracking, and controlling activities in his book, *Essentials of Software Project Management.*[2] In my experience, such project management practices can increase the probability of success, but by themselves are not always sufficient. I have seen projects where such practices were in use, yet success was threatened because the project manager failed to understand what individuals needed to do their best project work. This human component of managing projects is where leading others comes into the picture.

I think of leading others as both different and additive to project management. While there may some overlap, project management generally is focused more on managing the project work. Leading others is focused more on ways of working with individuals so that they can do their best project work. My colleague Jerry Weinberg defines leadership as "…the process of creating an environment in which people become empowered."[3] This is an important way of leading others—by working on their environment.

---

[1]Meilir Page-Jones, *Practical Project Management* (New York: Dorset House Publishing, 1985), p. 61.

[2]Richard Bechtold, *Essentials of Software Project Management* (Vienna, VA: Management Concepts, Inc., 1999), p. 19.

[3]Gerald M. Weinberg, *Becoming a Technical Leader* (New York: Dorset House Publishing, 1986), p. 12.

How does a project leader create such an environment? I have seen how this works in real projects. For example, on one seriously troubled project, a change of project leaders marked the beginning of a turnaround. The new project leader put into place feedback loops, which had not previously existed. The feedback loops, which were really nothing more than standard, rhythmic status reports and team meetings, resulted in more timely and relevant information being shared across the entire project. This environmental enhancement increased the quality and accessibility of project information. In turn, people were able to act more powerfully and responsibly—that is, they were *empowered*—because they had accurate and timely information to do their work.

While an empowering environment can be very helpful, some individuals may need more than that to become empowered. Most project leaders I know say that they want to work with empowered people. When I ask how empowered people act or what they do, here is how some describe their behavior:

- Act professionally
- Use good judgment
- Take their responsibilities seriously
- Collaborate well with other empowered people
- Take calculated risks
- Give honest feedback
- Behave ethically
- Follow up and follow through
- Have a passion for learning, especially about themselves
- See mistakes as a natural part of learning
- Aren't easily discouraged
- Are committed to the success of the project.

Unfortunately, project leaders may not always have a choice about who works on their projects. Typically, they will have a mix of individuals:

1. *Some individuals will already be empowered.* They will act powerfully and responsibly regardless of their environment. With these competent individuals, the project leader mostly just needs to stay out of their way. These individuals may need only minimal coaching or guidance because they are responsible, committed, and learning everything they need to know very quickly. This frees the project leader to work on enhancing the environment so that it supports and facilitates people doing their

best work. The project leader can also spend more time with a second type of individual.

2. *Some individuals may need or want help finding their power.* What I have come to believe through working with people is that everybody has within them everything they need to act empowered. When they do not act that way, there is a reason. These competent individuals may have become disconnected from their power, possibly due to a history of working for oppressive or abusive project leaders. For example, they may have felt punished for past attempts to act empowered and cannot muster the courage to try again. Or they may just be having a bumpy time, becoming stuck, or losing some confidence in themselves. Having an empowering environment can help these individuals, but each may want more direct help from the project leader to reconnect with his or her own power.

   Losing touch with one's power can happen to anyone at any time, even the individuals who are already empowered, and even to the project leader himself. Reconnecting with one's own power is not normally something one can do for oneself. Because of this, project leaders will need to be prepared by having someone else—a friend, peer, or mentor perhaps—to rely on for this kind of help when they lose touch with their own power.
3. *Some individuals may have no interest or desire whatsoever to act powerfully or responsibly, even if they can.* They may perceive no practical benefit or advantage from doing so. For example, they may perceive no difference in salary, promotions, and perks between those who act empowered and those who do not. These individuals may be competent or not. At a minimum, they will require close supervision, which can be a drain on everyone's time, especially the project leader's. After careful consideration, the project leader may need to show them the way off the project. In some cases, this can have the effect of enhancing the environment.

With regard to acting powerfully and responsibly, individuals can change. That is, empowered individuals can periodically get stuck or temporarily lose touch with their power. Individuals who are stuck can find their power again. Less frequently, individuals who have no interest or desire to act empowered can become interested—but it does happen.

The essence of leading others lies in working with individuals to help them tap into their own power and creating the conditions and the environment where they can work most effectively. This kind of "leading" consists of three abilities:

1. The ability to anticipate that each individual may need something different to do his or her best work.
2. The ability to work with each individual in such a way as to meet him where he is—not where you think he should be or where you wish he were—in terms of what he needs to do his best work. This may mean showing him off the project.
3. The ability to make an explicit agreement about what assistance you will provide and what he will do to get what he needs. What he needs may be anything, from an enhancement to his environment to help getting unstuck.

Leading others in this way may seem like a tall order. A project leader is supposed to be able to meet people where they are, find out what they need to do their best work and help them get it, and work on the environment to make it more empowering. Yes, it is a tall order. That is what the chapters in Part Two of this book are about. These chapters contain tips and techniques to help you get started leading others this way. After that, it takes practice, practice, practice.

Of course, while leading others, the project leader must also apply sound project management practices such as planning and organizing the project work. This book does not cover those practices, as they are covered quite well in the books by Page-Jones and Bechtold as well as in many other available books.

Chapter 7

LEADING FROM A HALF-STEP BEHIND

One technique to help you get started leading others in this way is what my colleague Jean McLendon, a therapist and organization development consultant, calls "leading from a half-step behind." I have seen Jean masterfully demonstrate this kind of leading. The usefulness of this technique transfers quite well from therapeutic settings to organizational and project settings. I have used it myself in many project consulting engagements. Briefly, here is the general form of how it works.

THE TECHNIQUE OF LEADING FROM A HALF-STEP BEHIND

With permission, the leader stands slightly behind and to the side of the person he is leading so that they are both facing the same direction. This can also be done sitting. Seeing this, one could imagine that they are both facing the question or problem to be explored together. Let us call that person the explorer. You could call him a programmer, or software engineer if you like. I use explorer because it conveys the sense of investigation, discovery, and learning that is the intent of this kind of leading. The leader "shines his flashlight" out in front of the explorer. Shining his flashlight is a metaphor for helping the explorer see some possible options to explore. The leader does this by asking questions and by commenting on what he is seeing and hearing from the explorer.

For example, suppose a software developer feels stuck and is not sure what kind of help to ask for. This would not be unusual. If he knew what kind of help to ask for, he might be able get himself unstuck. Nevertheless, assume that he asks the leader for some time to talk about it.

When they get together, the leader will make contact with the explorer by reconfirming the purpose of their talk and that both are ready to begin. Making contact is a necessary step in establishing a human connection and creating safety. The leader might do this by saying something like, "I understand that you want to talk about being stuck. Is that right? After confirming the purpose, the leader might say, "I am glad that you are here and that you came to me to talk about being stuck." (He should say this only if it is true, of course.) Next the leader might say, "Now that you are here, how do you feel about being here with me to talk about being stuck? The answer could be anything from "good" to "nervous" to "hopeful." The leader may want to probe to find out if feeling nervous, for example, is okay or if anything needs to be done about the nervousness before beginning. Finally, the leader may say, "Are you ready to begin?" Everything to this point has been about making contact.

Rather than start by asking the developer what kind of help he wants—a question the developer may not be able to answer at that moment—the leader might shine his flashlight by asking a question like, "What can you tell me about your stuckness?" In doing so, the leader has illuminated an option—a place to start the exploration.

The explorer, not the leader, decides which (if any) options to explore. This kind of leading always leaves the explorer in charge of himself. The leader does not tell the explorer what is right or true for the explorer, even if he thinks he knows. The point is for the explorer to find his or her own truth. The leader's job is to shine the flashlight periodically, stay in touch with the explorer's energy by listening and watching closely, and make sure that the explorer is supported. It is acceptable to ask the explorer a question like, "Is there anything you need right now to help you continue?" The answer could be anything from a drink of water to a lucky t-shirt to a few deep breaths. The leader should try to provide whatever is requested for support before continuing.

Leading from a half-step behind is a technique that you can add to your existing project leadership toolkit. By now in your project leadership career, you probably have developed your own ways of leading others that work for you. I am not suggesting that you replace your ways with leading from a half-step behind. There may be many times when you will have to assert your own wisdom to make difficult project decisions and give directions to your project team. In these situations, you should use whatever leadership techniques you know that work best for you.

There may also be times when you want to learn something that can come only from inside the individuals you lead. For example, before you can create an empowering environment, you will need to find out what individuals need to do their best work and what disempowers them. You will need to find out where their energy lies and where it does not. Before you can help individuals get unstuck or reconnect with their power, you will need to be able to guide and support them while they untangle these problems for themselves. It is not very helpful to command people to get unstuck or to tell them to "get over it." In these situations, you may need a technique like leading from a half-step behind that enables you to work with individuals in the following helpful ways:

- Make human contact with them.
- Leave them in charge of themselves.
- Guide rather than command their exploration with their full permission.
- Become a supportive partner in their learning process.
- Help them learn things about themselves that perhaps can be learned in no other way.
- Follow their energy.
- Enhance their self-esteem and yours.
- Encourage their creativity.

Let see how this technique could be applied to help Robert in the example of the rogue project manager, repeated here for convenience from Part One, Leading Yourself.

APPLYING THE TECHNIQUE: THE ROGUE PROJECT MANAGER

Robert is a project director in the IT services organization of a large corporation. His project is a multiyear, multimillion dollar ERP system project approaching go-live for a major component of that system.

Robert has a project manager reporting to him (one of four) for purposes of the project, but who reports functionally to another executive. Let's call her Alice. Her responsibility is the human resources module, which includes payroll. Robert perceives Alice to be difficult to work with, and he is concerned about her module. She will not give him status reports on time. She always has an excuse for missing project team meetings.

The other three project managers coordinate their efforts with each other. They keep Robert informed. They do not know what Alice's team is doing and vice versa. She seems to be taking her team in a different direction from the other teams. Robert has tried talking with her directly about his concerns. She won't talk with him about what's happening. Robert has discussed this situation with Alice's functional boss. There has been no change that he can observe.

Finally, in desperation, Robert goes to the project's two senior executive sponsors. He presents his concerns regarding the apparent disconnection between Alice's team and the other teams. Somehow these two executives don't perceive the problem to be important enough to show up on their radar screen. "It's just a personality issue," they say. "Work it out with her." As he leaves he says, "You bet." Inside, Robert is feeling alone and unsupported. His stomach is in a knot. He sucks up all the responsibility because this is what he does when he does not know what else to do. He does this unconsciously.

Robert tries to keep the other three teams informed the best he can. The ERP system is tightly integrated and the modules are interdependent. This requires close coordination among the project teams. Alice continues to act as though she does not report to Robert. Her team becomes isolated and disconnected from the rest of his project teams. Her team literally splits off from the other teams and becomes a separate project. Robert gives up and lets them.

Several months later, after go-live, the impact of this problem becomes very visible. The lack of coordination between Alice's team and the technical infrastructure team results in serious execution and data errors. User confidence is severely damaged because users were not prepared for the required changes in how they do their work. Some of the expected functionality of the implemented system is not available. This surprised users because they were not involved in testing the functionality. All these impacts can be directly related to increasing project cost by millions of dollars. There is plenty of blame, most of it finding its way to Robert.

What was happening?

Robert had gradually lost his ability to lead himself. He was not aware of, nor was he using, his own power. He was stuck. His needs for information, structure, and project oversight were not being considered in any way that he could notice. His letting Alice's team run wild was neither respectful nor caring of any of the four teams, the users, or the executive sponsors. It was also not caring of himself. It was an unconscious, automatic response, not a mindful one. Robert's behavior was inappropriate for the project's context—tightly integrated software and data among modules, which required users to change how they do their work. Such tight integration and business process changes required the four project teams to coordinate their efforts closely.

How might leading from a half-step behind help Robert find his power and get unstuck?

Robert's boss, let's call him Tom, could use the technique in the following ways:

Discover and articulate Robert's deeper concerns. After making contact with Robert, Tom might ask, "What concerns you about Alice's behavior?" Robert might initially answer by commenting on her refusal to cooperate with the other project managers, or take his direction, or give him accurate information. Tom could probe a little deeper by asking, "How does all that make you feel?" Robert might say, "Mad as hell. She is not being responsible." Tom could say, "I hear in your voice something really important about responsibility. Are you saying that responsibility is important to you? Robert might say, "I learned that I should always be responsible." Tom could ask, "Are you saying that Alice should always be responsible too?" Robert might say, "Well, I never thought about it like that, but yes, I suppose that's what I mean." Tom could say, "Setting aside for the moment that you and Alice might have learned different ways of being responsible, what could happen if Alice is not being responsible? Robert might say, "The project could be at serious risk." Tom could say, "That sounds very serious. Please tell more about the risks you see." At this point, Tom and Robert—perhaps for the first time—start to understand Robert's deeper concerns as he articulates the project risks he sees.

Acknowledge Robert's feelings about not being heard and explore other ways of being heard. Tom could ask, "What have you done to raise your concerns?" Robert might say, "I talked to Alice. I told Alice's functional boss. I told both executive project sponsors. Nobody seems to care." Tom could ask, "How does that make you feel that nobody seems to care?" Robert might say, "I feel alone and unsupported. Like I have to do it all by myself." Tom could say, "Let me check something with you. When you spoke with Alice's functional boss and the executive project sponsors, did you tell them about the serious risks to the project or only that you weren't getting Alice's cooperation?" Robert might say, "I only told them about Alice not cooperating. Yikes, I see now that I should have told them about the risks!" Tom could say, "Robert, I wonder if by making this about Alice instead of the project, you were unknowingly asking them to take sides with you against Alice. Do you think they might hear you more clearly now if you talked to them about project risks? Robert might say, "I think so. I'm going to try again."

Get clear about what Robert really wants to have happen. Tom could say, "Let me check something with you. You seem clearer now in your own mind about what is concerning you. You have another way to try to be heard and get support. Am I correct?" Robert might say, "Yes, you are correct." Tom could ask, "What do you really want to have happen? I think it would help to be clear about this when you go back to management to ask for their support." Robert might say with conviction, "I really want to replace Alice and I want my management to support me in that decision." Tom could say, "You sound very clear about that."

Get clear about what support Robert wants. Tom could ask, "Is there anything you want from me to help you with your next steps?" Robert might say, "I might want your advice on who to go to with my decision to replace Alice. And also how to present it." Tom could say, "Thank you for asking. I would be happy to help. Do you want my advice now or later?" Robert might say, "Thank you very much. Let me think about. I will let you know."

Obviously, this dialogue could go on, but I hope this is enough so you can see how it works. Tom used the technique to help Robert better understand his "stuckness" and see a way out. Robert knew deep inside what he wanted to have happen, but Tom helped him see how to do it in a powerful and responsible way. Being stuck is like that sometimes. At some level, perhaps just out of our awareness, we know what we want to do. But we just cannot see how to do it.

It takes practice—and self-awareness—to develop the level of skill Tom demonstrates here, and to take the kind of role that he does with Robert. In this way, learning to act powerfully is similar to learning and effectively applying technical project management skills. Self-awareness is what you develop over time by working with yourself—repeatedly doing the exercises under "Try This" in Part One, and going back to problem areas for you. Remember that it is okay—in fact, it is part of the learning process—to "stumble" or make mistakes.

The resources listed in Appendix A, Workshops, and Appendix B, Bibliography, can help you increase your self-awareness and develop your skills. The work you do with yourself and in your interactions with others can reap great rewards in getting you and those you work with out of the "stuck," seemingly hopeless places and creating an environment of empowerment.

To recap:

- Leading others is not a substitute for project management.
- A project manager, in addition to planning, tracking, and controlling project work, needs to have ways of creating an empowering environment and working with individuals so that they can do their best project work.
- The essence of leading others consists of three abilities:
  1. The ability to anticipate that each individual may need something different to do his or her best work.
  2. The ability to work with each individual in such a way as to meet him where he is—not where you think he should be or where you

wish he were—in terms of what he needs to do his best work. This might mean showing him off the project.

3. The ability to make an explicit agreement about what assistance you will provide and what he will do to get what he needs. What he needs may be anything from an enhancement to his environment to help getting unstuck.

- Leading from a half-step behind is useful when what you want to learn can only come from inside the individual you are leading, such as what motivates him or what he needs to do his best project work.

Try this:

1. Either privately or in a group discussion, think of five specific situations where leading from a half-step behind might be appropriate in your current project. How might this way of leading others help in those five situations?
2. Either privately or in a group discussion, think of five specific situations where leading from a half-step behind might not be appropriate in your current project. How might this way of leading others hinder these situations?
3. Write down five things that you need to do your best project work. How many do you have fully in your current project? How might you get the ones missing or get more of the ones you have only partially?
4. If you are leading a project now, do you really know (versus think you know) what each individual on your project team needs to do his or her best project work? If so, how do you know?

Chapter 8

WHAT DO PEOPLE NEED TO HELP THEM LEARN?

One answer to this question of what people need to help them learn is that each individual may need different things. But "learn what?" you might ask. Let's backtrack a bit.

The short answer is how to solve technical, process, and people problems. When projects get into trouble, the problems are often initially expressed as technical problems. For example, one might hear that tests are not catching enough bugs, reviews are not detecting enough defects, the gap analysis is taking too long, designs are not being approved soon enough, the requirements keep changing, the database response time is too slow, and so on. In reality, each of these problems usually has a process component and a people component, in addition to a technical component.

The technical component of these problems is often the most understood and perhaps the most interesting to technical people, and therefore may not pose as great a need for learning. Your technical people likely already possess the skills they need to solve the technical component of project problems.

The process and people components of these problems, however, are often the least understood, and therefore offer greater opportunities for learning. It is often not even clear who is responsible for solving the process and people components of project problems. But these components have real effects on projects.

THE TECHNICAL COMPONENT

As a project leader, you probably expect the individuals on your project team to be able to perform the core technical skills required to do their assigned jobs. For example, you might expect that:

- Business analysts can translate user requirements for the required information systems into technical specifications for developers.
- Programmers can code in the required language for the required platform.
- Testers can plan, construct, and perform the required tests.
- Database administrators can install, administer, secure, tune, and backup and recover the required databases.
- Network engineers can design and implement the required networks.
- Network administrators can administer the required networks and network applications.

When your reality does not match your expectations, you may have to take immediate action. Some individuals may have to develop their skills quickly by, for example, taking training courses or pairing with a more skilled team member.[1] So one answer to the question, "Learn what?" is how to solve the technical component of project problems.

THE PROCESS COMPONENT

But even when all individuals on the team are competent in the required core technical skills, projects can still get into trouble. Most of the troubled projects I see do not get into trouble because of technical problems. There may be a technical problem, but I see projects get into bigger trouble because of process problems.

By process, I simply mean *how* people do what they do. There are hundreds of processes in an organization, whether they are formalized and managed by process improvement techniques or informal and ad hoc. For example, there are processes for filling an open position on your project, hiring a contractor, purchasing capital equipment, initiating a project, changing the scope of the project, and so on. Here are two examples of the most frequent process problems I see on troubled projects:

- *Decision-making problems*: Decision-making is not treated like a process. The way that decisions get made is unclear and not

[1]You may also find that some individuals cannot acquire the skills quickly enough to meet the needs of the project—or do not seem to want to. In this case, you will have to replace them with individuals who have the necessary skills. It is important not to simply wait and hope the skills will materialize. Remember to stay connected to your internal resources so you have the wisdom and strength to take this difficult action—perhaps the wisdom box or the courage stick.

documented. Decisions are often either not made or take too long to make, and when made, do not stick. Decision criteria often do not exist, and if they do exist, decision-makers do not share the same understanding of them. Who makes decisions is often vague. Sometimes it is not clear when a decision has been made because decisions are not documented. There often is no differentiation among decisions as to which organization level is most appropriate to make a decision. There is no escalation process to handle disputes or misunderstandings about a particular decision. There is no follow-up to ensure that decisions are being carried out properly.

One effect that decision-making problems can have on projects is that important work can become stalled or accomplished out of sequence, impacting schedules. Another effect is that decisions can default to people who are not prepared to make informed decisions. On one project, important automated workflow decisions were defaulting to coders because decisions could not be obtained from the affected user management.

- *Inability to observe process*: This is an example of a meta process problem. By meta process, I mean the process of observing process. When people are not able to observe what they are doing, they can fail to notice process problems.

  One organization wanted to bring a service that had previously been outsourced in-house because of some disagreement with the outsourcer about the fee for the service at contract renewal time. The service had a significant software component. This organization had no previous experience with software development of any kind. The organization had no one who could competently hire or manage a software vendor. Nevertheless, a vendor was contracted to develop the software component of the service. After the vendor failed to produce the software in the specified time, the contact was terminated. The organization then hired its own programmers to develop the software even though no one in the organization was competent to hire or manage programmers. There was also no one skilled in project management. The hired programmers were also unable to produce the software in the specified time. When my partner and I got involved, the organization was about to hire another vendor.

  What this organization could not see was that it was stuck in a repeating cycle. The organization kept doing the same things over and over expecting different results. They thought the solution was to hire another vendor. With our help, they were

> able to see the cycle they were in and how they had perpetuated it for three years. The organization was eventually able to understand that unless they changed what *they* were doing, there was no reason to believe that the next attempt would be any more successful that the previous two.

So another answer to the question, "Learn what?" is how to solve the process component of project problems. Most individuals probably do not arrive on your project already having learned to diagnose and solve process problems, unless they have been specially trained in that discipline.

THE PEOPLE COMPONENT

By far the biggest trouble I see on projects comes from people problems. Again, most people on your project team probably are not trained to diagnose and solve people problems. So another answer to the question, "Learn what?" is how to solve the people component of project problems. The ways that individuals cope and behave can become potential people components of project problems when, for example:

- Their expectations are unmet.
- Their perceptions differ.
- They feel overcome with strong emotions.
- They have puzzling interactions with one another.
- They have difficulty negotiating for their wants or needs.
- They are working with others who are very different from themselves.

Here are few examples of people problems.

Bill's work ethic will not permit him to give less than 100 percent. He notices that others on his project do not appear to work as hard as he does and they do not seem to care about the quality of their work. Bill has trouble keeping his motivation up and is starting to feel taken for granted. He resents the project leader's apparent acceptance of this situation and wonders why she does not do something about it. He starts searching for another project where his work ethic will be more appreciated and more closely matched with that of his teammates.

Tammy works in production operations. She is assigned to the Sapphire project for 50 percent of her time. She negotiated with her boss and Chris, the Sapphire project leader, that her first priority is production operations problems. Chris is upset with Tammy because she has not attended the past two staff meetings, and she is two days late on completing a task. Tammy's reason is that there has been a rash of production problems that demanded her immediate attention. Tammy, her production operations boss, and Chris are upset with one another and are arguing over priorities. Chris apparently failed to plan for the fact that even though she had 50 percent of Tammy's time, production problems could take Tammy away from the project at any time. Meanwhile, the Sapphire project slips behind schedule.

Max is a user representative from the human resources department. He is a payroll specialist. Max had been involved in the design and testing of his department's current home-grown payroll system 20 years ago and since then has been involved in all major enhancements.

The IT department is now replacing all the human resources systems, including payroll, with a new integrated system from a well-known vendor. This modernization project is called the IHRMS project. The IHRMS project leader, Kathy, solicited input from Max to help with the user interface and workflow design. Max has made several attempts to give his input, but each time Betty, the person designated by Kathy to receive the input, postpones their meeting. Max documents his input in writing and emails it to Betty; he cc's Kathy, asking for a ping back to confirm receipt. Max notices that decisions have been made regarding the user interface and workflow. He has yet to receive any confirmation that his input has been received, and he cannot see any evidence in the decisions that his input has had any effect.

Now, six months have passed and the IHRMS project is in the user acceptance-testing phase. The payroll department users participating in the testing are frustrated and on the warpath. IHRMS has been unable to produce even one acceptable payroll test result. The human resources director does not recognize the IHRMS work flow and refuses to approve it. Kathy is furious and blames HR for sabotaging her project.

Jim reports to Ed. Ed is really into details. When Ed wants a status report on Jim's project, he expects details. He perceives what he gets from Jim to be an overview, too high-level to be useful. Jim gets defensive when Ed presses for details. Jim interprets Ed's insistence on details as micro management. To Ed, "The project is on track" is not sufficient. He wants to know how many tasks were scheduled to be completed, how many were actually completed, what the recovery plan is for any that were not completed, the actual versus budgeted hours to date, and a review of the current top five project risks. Ed wonders if Jim is really the right person for the job. Jim is searching for a boss who is more trusting and gives him lots of freedom

Allen reports to Victor. Victor prefers a big-picture overview. When Victor wants a status report on Allen's project, he expects an overview. He perceives what he gets from Allen to be too detailed. Allen perceives that Victor gets impatient and becomes short with him. Allen interprets Victor's interest in his project to be superficial. He thinks a good manager ought to want to know the details. How else could Victor make informed decisions? To Victor,

"The project is on track" is sufficient; he trusts Allen. But Allen wants Victor to know how many tasks were scheduled to be completed, how many were actually completed, what the recovery plan is for any that were not completed, the actual versus budgeted hours to date, and a review of the current top five project risks. Allen and Victor are puzzles to each other. Allen is searching for a "better" boss. Victor will be caught off guard when Allen quits.

In each of these stories, a project was or will be significantly impacted because the individuals did not know any other ways to resolve their problems with each other. The individuals in these examples are not bad or incompetent people. They did the only thing they knew to do at the time. Projects can benefit when people learn to solve their problems with one another in ways that offer more choices for understanding and connecting instead of misinterpreting, resenting, blaming, arguing, writing people off, or leaving.

THE PROJECT LEADER'S ROLE IN HELPING PEOPLE LEARN

I have repeatedly been emphasizing the importance of learning—about self, about others, and about your project's context. One of your most important roles as a project leader is teacher. A good teacher of adults will ask, "What do my adult learners need to do their best learning?" The answer will of course depend on the individual. No one can answer that question for any individual as well as that individual can. A good teacher will help his adult learners construct their own knowledge rather than try to pour his knowledge into their heads.

A project leader may not be responsible for teaching individuals how to diagnose and solve the process and people components of project problems. But a project leader can help his project immensely by creating a project environment in which individuals can learn how to solve these kinds of problems if they want to.

The people who want to learn these things often have a passion for learning, especially about themselves. These people usually want to go beyond the minimum learning necessary. They want to go deeper than just knowledge. They want to apply the knowledge and develop their skills. These qualities are very important in learning how to solve process and people problems. To solve these problems, individuals have to be willing to see themselves as part of the problem and the solution, and possibly change themselves.

In the role of teacher, the project leader will try to:

- Find out who wants to learn how to solve process and people problems.

- Find out what those people need to do their best learning.
- Create an environment that makes it easier for them to learn.

SOME NORMS THAT MAKE IT EASIER FOR PEOPLE TO LEARN

The first step in creating an environment that makes it easier for people to learn is to identify who wants to learn. The next step is to find out what each individual needs to do his or her best learning. The simplest—and best—approach is to ask each person directly. Every person may not know how to answer this immediately. In this case, some flexibility and patience while the person figures it out only increase the safety of the environment. Working with the energy of the people who want to learn—not against the energy of the people who do not want to learn—will be less tiring for everybody.

Establishing a few norms can add some structure to the environment. A norm is a standard for behavior within a group. Norms can emerge on their own over time implicitly to describe how people behave in a group. Norms can also be created explicitly when a group is just forming to describe how people want to behave. What individuals say they need to do their best learning can be a start to creating the norms. It is best if the norms are created and accepted using a consensus process.

Here are a several examples of what I mean by norms. This collection comes from many different "learning communities" of which I have been a member:

- We acknowledge that each individual may need different things to help him or her learn.
- We allow each individual the freedom to learn in his preferred way.
- We understand and accept that temporary incompetence is a necessary part of the learning process.
- We take risks to try, and we learn from failure.
- We appreciate openness and disclosure.
- We welcome and invite feedback.
- Each of us is in charge of ourselves.
- We view invitations to take risks as helpful.
- We listen to each other.
- We speak only for ourselves.
- Our goal is high self-esteem for each of us.
- We check with someone first to see if he or she wants help before we start helping.

- We respect individual needs for space and support when learning a new skill.
- We allow ourselves the freedom to learn at different speeds.
- We view having fun and being serious as both valid while learning.
- When we are curious, we ask questions.
- We can change these norms whenever we need to as long as everyone agrees.

It never ceases to amaze me how creative and productive people can be when they work in an environment where individuals respect each other and accept their differences—whether they be race, religion, sexual preference, gender, politics, or any other diversity one can imagine. I have experienced this creativity and productivity myself and always feel grateful for it.

To recap:

- When projects get into trouble, the problems are often initially expressed as technical problems. In reality, each of these problems usually has a process component and a people component in addition to a technical component.
- The process and people components of project problems are often the least understood, and therefore they may offer greater opportunities for learning. For example, it is often not even clear who is responsible for solving the process and people components of project problems.
- As a project leader, you probably expect the individuals on your project team to be able to perform the core technical skills required to do their assigned job. For example, you may expect that programmers can code in the required language for the required platform. When your reality does not match your expectations, however, you may have to take immediate action. Some individuals may have to develop their skills quickly so they can solve the technical component of project problems.
- The process component of project problems is about *how* people do what they do. For example, how decisions are made is a process. Decision-making is a frequent process component of project problems.
- The people component of project problems is often the component that causes the biggest trouble for projects. The ways that individuals cope and behave when their expectations are unmet, their perceptions differ, they feel overcome with strong emotions, they have puzzling interactions with one another, they must negotiate for their wants

or needs, and they are working with others who are very different from themselves can become potential people components of project problems.

- The role of the project leader in helping people learn is to find out who wants to learn how to solve process and people problems, find out what those people need to do their best learning, and then create an environment that makes it easier for them to learn.
- One way to create an environment that makes it easier for people to learn is to establish a few norms. A norm is a standard for behavior within a group. For example, "We listen to each other" can be a norm.

Try this:

1. Have a team discussion during which individuals talk about what they need to do their best learning.
2. Create a "strength reminder list" for yourself and your team. Have a brainstorming session with your team. Start by having one person volunteer to be the star. (Each person will have an opportunity to be the star.) The others who are not the star brainstorm a list of the star's strengths and admirable qualities. The strengths and qualities are captured on a flip chart or in some other way. The brainstorming is done in the presence of the star, but the star does not participate or comment until the brainstorming stops. For example, during the brainstorming, the star is not permitted to argue that he or she does not possess a particular strength or quality.

   When the brainstorming stops, the star may be invited to say what his or her reactions are to the list. The star is also permitted to add to the list anything that seems to be missing, but not to remove any items from the list. Then another person volunteers to be the star and so on until everyone has had an opportunity to be the star.

   Each person should receive a copy of his or her list to keep. Optionally, a group list containing all the individual lists may be created and kept by each person in the group. At any time when an individual starts to doubt himself, feel uncertain about his worth, or need a self-esteem boost, he can pull out the strength reminder list and read it. He might even put a copy of this list in with his survival kit, if your team members have been introduced to this concept.

Chapter 9
EVERYTHING THAT HAPPENS IS AN OPPORTUNITY FOR LEARNING

On projects there is always a need and an opportunity to learn. By "learn," I mean ascertain, change, detect, discover, experiment, find out, investigate, master, observe, pick up, research, review, study, and test. All these verbs typically involve learning of some kind, either as a process or as an objective. For example, a project review is a process for learning about the real status of the project. A specific learning objective of a project review might be to find out how the top three risks to the project are being managed. Project teams that approach projects as opportunities for learning seem to be more creative in solving problems and more successful in achieving project objectives.

Some people have a passion for learning, especially about themselves, and projects need such people. Projects can be like living laboratories where passionate learners can find the learning opportunities they seek from everything that happens all around them. I believe that understanding how one's "family rules" can be a potential hindrance to learning on projects, and how to transform those rules into flexible guides, is a key to project success.

PROJECTS: LIVING LEARNING LABORATORIES

Some people are not satisfied with knowing the minimum necessary to get by. They want to learn the finer points of their subject matter. They want to delve deeper into their subject matter. They seek mastery. Where do they go to get satisfaction? After they absorb all the notable books and complete every available training course on their topic of interest, where is their next opportunity to learn?

We do not have to enroll in a conference or workshop, or even purchase a book, to find learning opportunities. We need only to seize the opportunities that are around us all the time. We pay tuition for these opportunities whether we get the learning or not. The tuition we pay is day-to-day, second-to-second in the form of disappointment, embarrassment, shame, stress, strained relationships, lost productivity, career bumps and bruises, unmet longings, and so forth. Perhaps if we could capture more of the learning available, we might be able to gradually lower the tuition.

So, one answer to where is the next opportunity to learn is: *Everything that happens is an opportunity for learning*. Real-time project situations can provide passionate learners with a living laboratory to deepen their knowledge and skill. Instead of classroom case studies or exercises, they seize opportunities from everything that happens around them to expand the edges of their expertise.

For example, a competent C++ programmer who is a passionate learner may look for opportunities to apply his coding skills with many different kinds of hardware platforms, operating systems, types of applications, industries, sizes of projects, and personalities of other programmers and project managers. He may appreciate the stretch beyond just knowing how to code C++ to working with C++ in many different kinds of situations. He may appreciate the stretch because it requires of him more than a mastery of coding C++. It requires the ability to manage his own stress reactions and responses, to manage his interactions with other project members, and to understand the context in which his expertise is being applied.

A powerful project leader understands the need for learning on projects and the desire of passionate learners to learn. He will encourage the attitude that *everything is an opportunity for learning* as a project norm. For example, some project leaders may consider stress reactions of individuals and emotional bumps between team members to be annoying and may try to ignore these reactions and bumps. A powerful project leader will treat them as opportunities for the individuals to learn—about themselves and about working with each other—and for himself to learn more about helping others learn.

Here is a story from a real client situation of how stress and difficult communications stalled a project.

Imagine that you are the project leader of a development team that is working on a very tight (read impossible) schedule to complete a new product offering–code name Sisyphus. Your management has decided that Sisyphus should be developed using a specific development environment–code name Ruby. Ruby is not released yet. Another team in a different geographical location is developing it. The Ruby development team is part of the company that recently acquired your company.

You have arranged a couple of videoconferences for technical information exchange between your Sisyphus team and the Ruby team. The videoconferences are bizarre. Everyone just sits there in silence. The Ruby team seems to be waiting for your team to ask questions. Your team asks what you perceive to be only superficial questions. They claim they do not know enough to ask intelligent questions, but cannot seem to tell you what they would need to know so they could. You ask the Ruby team what you think are a couple of helpful questions to get a discussion started. The Ruby team responds by saying, "Uh, we're not that far along yet. When we figure it out, we'll get back to you." Your project is stalled.

In this situation, a lot is happening and a lot is not happening. What is not happening, if we can train ourselves to notice this, can be an opportunity for learning. There are many things that need to be learned very quickly for this project to be successful. In this case, important *technical information exchange* is not happening. Some of the people in the real situation had received training in interpersonal communication, team building, conflict management, and relevant technical topics at various times in their careers. But they seemed unable to access what they had learned. Perhaps it was because a project context is not the same as a classroom context. Perhaps it was because their training was more technique-focused and less self-focused, leaving them unprepared and confused by their own stress reactions and responses.

The Sisyphus project leader reframed the situation as an opportunity to practice and deepen his team's understanding of what they already knew about working with others, and added some new learning focused on self to help them know what to do with their stress reactions. One of the things he did was to change the focus from looking at the problem—technical information exchange—to looking at how his team was coping with the problem. He and his team had several group discussions about how each individual had been coping with the problem and how well the coping had worked to that point. Through these discussions, the team members began to realize how vulnerable they felt and how stressful it was to feel vulnerable. They talked about what support they needed from each other and from the Ruby team to address their vulnerabilities. They also acknowledged that the Ruby team might also be feeling vulnerable and were open to the idea that the Ruby team might need support from them as well.

The Sisyphus team was eventually able to make contact with the Ruby team on the basis of needs and vulnerabilties instead of who has the right to tell whom what to do or who owns what information. This completely transformed the relationship between the two teams. Using this real project situation, the Sisyphus team leader helped his team members first learn something about themselves. This new self-awareness cleared the way for his team to access and use what they had previously learned about interpersonal communication, team building, and conflict management. His team responded well to the learning opportunity and the technical information began to flow.

Other project opportunities to learn might include how to:

- Work with a new methodology
- Work with a new technology
- Work with a new programming language
- Work with a person new to you
- Work with a new client
- Work with a new vendor
- Work with another project team whose culture, first language, and time zone are different from yours
- Work with management from the new company that just acquired your company.

FAMILY RULES

Most of us learned a lot of rules when we were growing up. Our parents and other grownups gave us rules to keep us safe from dangers we were not prepared to handle on our own. Some rules may have been given to socialize us—to teach us how to "get along" in the world. Some of our rules may be out of our awareness. If we are aware of them at all, our conscious mind may recognize them in their short, not-so-rigid form. Subconsciously, they typically have a longer, much more rigid form. In practice, we try to behave according to the long form. See if you recognize any of these examples of family rules in short form:

- Be responsible.
- Don't depend on anyone else.
- Be in control.
- Never volunteer.
- Be perfect.
- Don't fail.
- Be strong.
- Do what you believe is right, no matter what.
- Be nice.
- Have the last word.
- Don't ask for anything for yourself.
- Don't confront anyone directly.
- Don't draw attention to yourself.
- Work hard and you will succeed.

The short form of these rules does not seem to be all that rigid. However, the long form—the one that can subconsciously drive our behavior—is very rigid. Here are a couple of examples to show you the contrast:

Short form: Be responsible.
Long form: I must always be responsible for everything.

Short form: Don't fail.
Long form: I must never fail.

Short form: Have the last word.
Long form: I must always have the last word.

Short form: Be perfect.
Long form: I must always be perfect.

Now that we are grownups—some of us are parents ourselves—our rules are still with us like frozen knowledge (unless we somehow changed them before now). Rules are often first given to cover a specific context, but then become generalized over time. The context often becomes part of the memory of this rule. That is why you cannot know the full significance of anyone else's rule even if you have the same or similar rule. For example, I have a rule that I must always pay my own way. I remember precisely when I received this rule.

I was six years old. I went to the school carnival with my classmate buddy. My mom gave me some money to buy ride tickets. My classmate's mom gave him money to buy tickets too. We had a blast. We rode some rides together, others separately. I ran out of tickets before my classmate did and before it was time to go. My classmate still had lots of tickets left, so he gave me some of his. Later when my mom came to take me home, I told her about how much fun I had. I told her about how my classmate shared his tickets with me. What happened next took me completely by surprise. My mom started yelling at me and jerking my arm. She screamed, "You should know better than to accept tickets you didn't pay for. You should pay for your own tickets, and if you can't, then you shouldn't ride. I don't want you mooching off others." She dragged me around by the arm until she found my classmate and his mother. She insisted on paying my classmate's mother for the tickets I "mooched." I was mortified. That's the day I got the rule, *I must always pay my own way.*

The problem with rules is that they cannot fit every situation; thus, it is impossible and inhuman for us to expect ourselves to follow them all the time. But many of us try to live by them anyway, and then feel guilty or angry because we have them. What we need are guides, not rules. Our rules can be relentless bosses. Without giving up the old rules, we can add some new possibilities—and thereby loosen the grip a bit.

Transforming rules into guides can add flexibility to our learning. A good place to start looking for your rules is your list of *shoulds*. Your shoulds are the things you do or do not do because that little voice inside says you should. We all have shoulds.

I have provided several categories of rules below, stated in their long form and matched with some possible shoulds. There are, of course, lots of other possible shoulds. I chose these rule categories because I think they have potential to prevent you from taking opportunities to learn in real-time project situations. For example, a rule like *you must never depend on anyone else* might prevent you from learning how to solve a particular kind of problem when you cannot allow yourself to accept help. A rule like *you must always be fully responsible for everything* might prevent someone else from learning if you insert yourself too soon and take over. A rule like *you must always be logical* might prevent you from learning how to connect with other people on an emotional level when doing so could be helpful. A rule like *you must never fail* might prevent you from learning something new if you will not take a risk. A rule like *you must always be nice* might prevent you from learning how to stand up for your ideas against verbal bullies.

I have included the shoulds so that if you resonate with the rule (in italics), you can see what behavior could result. On the flip side, if you resonate with the should, you can see what rule might be driving it. The general form is: Because [*rule*] you should or shouldn't [behavior]. See if you resonate with any of these.

Rules about Responsibility

Because *you must always be fully responsible for everything*, you should insert yourself and take over when necessary.

Because *you must always keep your word*, you shouldn't make commitments you know you can't keep.

Because *you must always obey authority*, you should follow orders even when you think they're wrong.

Because *you must always pay your own way*, you shouldn't let your colleague pay for your lunch.

Because *you must never depend on anyone else*, you shouldn't accept any help if you cannot solve the problem yourself.

Because *you must never arrive first*, when attending meetings you should make sure someone else is in the room before you go in.

Because *you must never be late*, when attending meetings or appointments you should plan to arrive a few minutes early.

Because *you must never volunteer*, you should wait to be asked.

Rules about Control

Because *you must always be in control*, you shouldn't let people know you are upset.

Because *you must always be logical*, you should ignore your feelings and others' feelings.

Rules about Perfection

Because *you must always be perfect*, you shouldn't say or do anything in public unless you can do it perfectly.

Because *you must always know everything*, you should have a solution for every problem.

Because *you must never fail*, you shouldn't try something new that might fail.

Because *you must never fail*, you should avoid situations in which you might make a mistake. Mistakes mean failure.

Because *you must never admit you do not know something*, you shouldn't say, "I don't know."

Because *you must never admit you're wrong*, argue your point ad naseum, insisting that you're right.

Rules about Being Strong

Because *you must always be strong*, you shouldn't allow your tears to show. Crying will be seen as weak.

Because *you must always be strong*, you should pretend everything is okay, even when you feel hopeless.

Because *you must always do what you believe is right, no matter what*, it shouldn't bother you much if others are upset with your decision.

Rules about Commenting

Because *you must always have the last word*, you shouldn't back down.

Because *you must always be fair to everyone*, you should consider each person's feedback before you respond.

Because *you must always be nice*, you shouldn't say hurtful things to others even if you really want to.

Because *you must always speak first*, you should talk over others so you are heard.

Because *you must always take things seriously*, you shouldn't let your guard down. Life is hard.

Because *you must never speak first*, you should wait until someone else says what he or she thinks first.

Because *you must never ask for anything for yourself*, if you are the only one who has a question, you should let it go.

Because *you must never confront anyone directly*, if you don't agree, you should keep it to yourself.

Because *you must never draw attention to yourself*, you shouldn't tell what you know in public.

Because *you must never say what you're really feeling directly to the person involved*, you should pretend you are confident even when you aren't.

Because *you must always stick to the facts*, you shouldn't offer any of your opinions or brainstorm ideas.

Because *you must never talk to strangers*, you shouldn't share information with people you don't know well.

TRANSFORMING FAMILY RULES INTO GUIDES[1]

A rigid rule can be transformed into a flexible guide by taking the following steps. For example, the rule *never disagree in public* may be transformed as follows:

Step 1. Write or state the rule precisely in the following form:

I must never disagree in public.

Notice how rigid and absolute this sounds. If you were to try to live up to this rule, you could easily get ulcers or become sick in some other way. You may have to play around with the wording until you get it just right. For example, this rule could be worded slightly differently in several different ways:

I must never be disagreeable in public.

I must never argue in public.

I must never argue.

It is important to keep the "I must never (or always)" part. This is the part that makes the rule so rigid and unforgiving. It is also important to get the wording that matches your experience of the rule. On the surface, playing with these variations may seem trivial, but your memory of the rule will be triggered strongly when you hit the correct wording.

Step 2. Acknowledge and honor the rule.

Take whatever time you need to acknowledge ownership of the rule. For better or worse, this is your rule. Accept the positive intention the rule may have been meant to have when you got it. What might the positive intention have been? For example, the rule *I must never disagree in public* might have been meant to protect your privacy. Or perhaps it was meant to avoid embarrassment for you and the person with whom you disagree. If you do not go through this

---

[1]Virginia Satir, *Making Contact* (Berkeley: Celestial Arts, 1976).

step, you may find it very difficult to successfully navigate the next steps. Some rules may cause you so much trouble that you may think you want to get rid of them entirely. This does not usually work well. Psychologically, this can be tricky. Your mind may resist this. Modifying a rule slightly into a guide preserves instead of eliminates. This is often easier for your mind to accept.

Step 3. Change "must" to "can."

I can never disagree in public.

The word "must" suggests compulsion and no choice. The word "can" suggests choice. This step starts to loosen up the tight hold your rule may have on you by introducing the idea that you can—should you choose to—never disagree in public.

Step 4. Change "always" or "never" to "sometimes."

I can sometimes disagree in public.

This step loosens up the grip even more by introducing more choice. Absolutes like *always* and *never* suggest certainty. The word *sometimes* suggests possibility. This step introduces the idea that you can—should you choose to—sometimes—when you choose to—disagree in public.

Step 5. Select three or more situations that describe when you can disagree in public.

I can sometimes disagree in public when:

An important issue is being overlooked.

I feel strongly about something.

I do it in a respectful way.

This step moves you from the general case, which may be confusing in its vagueness, to specific situations in which you can disagree. With the completion of all five steps, the rigid, inhuman rule *I must never disagree in public* has been transformed into a flexible, human guide that can really be lived up to.

Understanding how family rules can hinder learning for people on your project (including yourself) is a goldmine of opportunity for those who are passionate about learning. Transforming rules into flexible guides opens up even more opportunities. For example, if instead of never accepting help from anyone, you can now accept help from some individuals in some situations, maybe you will solve the problem you previously could not solve. If you can let someone else be responsible sometimes, and not take over, that person will have an opportunity to learn something. When you tame your rules, you make them your learning partners.

To recap:

- On projects there is always a need and an opportunity to learn.
- Projects can be like living laboratories where passionate learners can find the learning opportunities they seek from everything that happens all around them.
- Opportunities for learning are around us all the time. We pay tuition for these opportunities whether we get the learning or not. The tuition we pay is day-to-day, second-to-second in the form of disappointment, embarrassment, shame, stress, strained relationships, lost productivity, career bumps and bruises, unmet longings, and so forth.
- Some project leaders may consider stress reactions of individuals and emotional bumps between team members to be annoying and may try to ignore these reactions and bumps. A powerful project leader will treat them as opportunities for the individuals to learn—about themselves and about working with each other—and for himself to learn more about helping others learn.
- Family rules can sometimes hinder our learning in real project situations. A rule like *you must never depend on anyone else* might prevent you from learning how to solve a particular kind of project problem when you cannot allow yourself to accept help.
- Rules are often first given to cover a specific context, but then become generalized over time.
- You cannot know the full significance of anyone else's rule even if you have the same or similar rule.
- The problem with rules is that they cannot fit every situation so it is impossible and inhuman for us to expect ourselves to follow them all the time.
- Transforming rules into guides can add flexibility to learning, such as when we are able to accept help in some situations, or when we can allow someone else to be responsible in some situations.

Try this:

1. My colleague Peter Hayward suggests you try this.[2] Observe how many opportunities for learning there are on your current project. Share and discuss your observations with your project leader.
2. Make a list of your shoulds and should nots. Using your list, see if you can discover any of your family rules.

[2]E-mail, August 20, 2001.

3. If you have difficulty making your list, use the list in this chapter to start with. If you find a rule that you think is close to one of yours, play with the words until it is clear to you that you have it just right.
4. My colleague Peter Hayward also suggests that, using your list of rules (or shoulds), see which ones may be affecting you on your current project.[3] Transform one of these rules and see how you act differently. Share this experience with another project member and see if he or she would be interested in trying the same exercise.

---

[3]E-mail, August 20, 2001.

Chapter 10

FINDING THE ENERGY

Have you ever tried to sign your name with your nondominant hand? Try it. I have done this signature writing exercise with hundreds of people. If you are like most people, you can do it, but it takes more energy and time. It usually does not look as good as if you had signed with your dominant hand, although sometimes people are surprised by how good it does look. Writing it feels awkward. You have to really concentrate on how to form the letters. I have timed groups both with dominant hand and nondominant hand signatures. On the first try it takes on average three times as long to sign your name with your nondominant hand.

On a small scale, this is what it is like to work against your energy. Imagine what it would be like to be on a project where day in and day out you worked against your energy. People who have done this exercise report that with their dominant hand, writing their signature is "effortless." "It just flows naturally." "It feels comfortable." On a small scale, this is what it is like to work with your energy. Imagine what it would be like to be on a project where day in and day out you worked with your energy.

What does this have to do with leading others? A powerful project leader knows how to *find the energy* of the individuals on his project team. Then he attempts to create a work environment that maximizes the natural attraction between the available work and the available energy. In this way, every individual is working (as much as possible) with his or her energy as opposed to against it.

Another name for energy is motivation. Different things can motivate each individual. Despite what you may have learned in a management course, motivation is not one-size-fits-all. Some managers use a threat/reward model of motivation. These managers operate as though they believe that employees do not have any natural motivation, so the only way to get them to comply is to threaten or reward them.

Managers who try to intimidate employees by threatening them may think that they are motivating them, but the opposite is true. When employees comply, it may look like their manager has motivated them. But compliance may come out of fear rather than motivation. A work environment based on fear and intimidation will eventually collapse because employees with high skill levels and high self-esteem will leave.

Managers who try to manipulate employees with rewards also fool no one. Smart employees will quickly see that such managers have to resort to this tactic because they know no other way of motivating. Rewards can be appropriate in some cases, but not when the intent is to manipulate an employee to do something he would not otherwise do.

Powerful project leaders do not resort to threat/reward tactics because they know how to create an environment that encourages employees' own natural motivation.

WHERE DOES ENERGY COME FROM?

The sources of energy can vary widely among individuals. For example, I tend to have the most energy when I perceive that what I am working on:

- Is interesting
- Is challenging
- Is acknowledged and appreciated
- Adds value.

My energy is less if the work is challenging but not interesting and vice versa. Likewise, if the work adds value, but is not interesting or challenging, then I have less energy for it. Of course, some things I do are not interesting or challenging, nor do they add value. I do those things even though my energy for doing them is low.

To keep myself motivated, I need challenge and some level of interest, with the right amount of each. The right amount of each is not a precisely known quantity. It changes over time. For example, when I have too much interesting and challenging work, I crave some boring, mind-numbing work. When I notice that craving, then I know that I have crossed a threshold. That is when I update my contacts database or balance my checkbook or trim the shrubs around my house.

HOW TO FIND THE ENERGY

When I review projects for my clients, one of the things I try to do is find the energy of the project team. I also look for more traditional project indicators, such as planned versus actual progress, scope management, and risk identification and management. Those indicators often mask both opportunities and threats to a project's success because they can be symptoms of underlying energy issues. For example, a highly motivated, energetic team may put its project at risk by accepting every scope change request without analyzing the impacts.

Begin by Making Contact

To find your project team's energy, begin by making contact with the individuals on your team. Do this by talking with people individually or in small groups. Start by setting the context. Set the context by stating the purpose of your inquiry and how you want to structure it, such as individual meetings. Create safety. People generally feel safer when they have choices, know the purpose, know how the information they give will be used, and know that there are no right or wrong answers to your questions.

One approach is to announce to everyone that you are looking for ideas about how to increase the quality of both their experience and yours during this project. Tell them you'd like to know from each of them what it's like working on this project from their perspective.

This kind of announcement may be unusual in your team culture. If so, acknowledge that. Tell them you will schedule time with them individually, and make it clear that what they talk about is completely their choice. Express appreciation to them in advance for taking their time to help you. Given the freedom and encouragement to do so—and if they feel safe enough—people will usually talk about what is important to them.

Ask "Energy" Questions

The usual project dashboard kinds of questions won't work. Those are questions about "things." For example, "What is the percent complete on each of your work packages versus planned percent complete?" is a question about progress. To find the energy, you need to ask *energy* questions.

Let's say you want to find where Colleen's energy is. Here are some examples of energy questions you could ask Colleen:

What do you enjoy most about working on this project?

The answer to this question can give you insight into what Colleen enjoys. People usually have lots of energy for doing what they enjoy. Do not try to anticipate the answer. Be open to what they have to say. The answer could be anything from, "I enjoy having my own parking space in the garage" to "I enjoy working with Marv" to "I really like analyzing requirements." Now it will be even more helpful to learn, for example, what it is about analyzing requirements that Colleen enjoys.

What is it about [analyzing requirements] that you enjoy?

This is a follow-on question. You fill in the part in brackets from the answer to the question, *What do you enjoy most about working on this project*? The answer can help you know more precisely what the source of Colleen's energy might be. For example, the answer might be, "It's interesting." Or, "It's really stretching me, and I'm learning a lot." Another possible answer might be, "I like bridging the gap between business people and technical people by translating business requirements into requirements that technical people can understand. When I am able to do that, I feel like I am contributing something really valuable." Do not judge the answers as right or wrong, good or bad. Consider them information, and appreciate that you now know something more about where Colleen's energy lies.

How much of your time do you spend [analyzing requirements]?

The answer can provide a baseline. If the answer were, say, 10 percent, I would definitely want to know how this might be affecting Colleen's energy. I could guess that 10 percent is not enough to sustain a high energy level, but it is wise to check this out. If the answer were 90 percent, I would still want to know how this might be affecting Colleen's energy. For some, 90 percent might be perfect. For others, 90 percent might be too much of a good thing.

What do you not enjoy about working on this project?

The answer to this question can give you insight into what Colleen does not enjoy. Generally, people have less motivation for work they do not enjoy than for work they do enjoy. The answer may be, "Nothing." Or it may be, "I really do not enjoy doing gap analysis of functional requirements to a packaged software application."

What is it about [gap analysis] work that you do not enjoy?

This is a follow-on question. The answer can help you know more precisely why Colleen does not enjoy gap analysis of functional requirements to a packaged software application. For example, the answer might be, "I do not like studying an existing system. It's boring. I much prefer to be involved in creating new software from scratch. It's fun to imagine different design scenarios, and try to guess how it will turn out."

How much of your time do you spend doing [gap analysis]?

The answer to this question also provides a baseline. If Colleen spends the majority of her time doing what she does not enjoy, you might want to check out with her how that is affecting her energy level. Colleen might say, "This project is totally about implementing a packaged software application. There are no new software development projects going on right now, so I guess this will do until one comes along."

You do not necessarily have to do anything with this information. In fact, there may be nothing you can do for this project. But now you know that you have a person on your project doing work she does not enjoy. This is something to be monitored. Be open to her ideas about how to make the work more energizing. Ask the next question.

If you could, what would you change about your work on this project?

The answer to this question can give you clues about how to create a more energizing work environment for Colleen. You may not be able to change anything for the moment, and you should be very clear about that with Colleen. You do not want to create any expectations that you will change the work environment. But if you could, then you would know what to change.

What do you think is working well on this project?

The answer to this question can give you information about Colleen's perspective of what is working well on your project. You do not have to agree or disagree. Consider it information, not necessarily fact. Accept it as Colleen's perspective, not necessarily anyone else's. You may or may not be surprised by the answer. Do not try to make Colleen justify her answer.

What concerns you most about this project?

The answer to this question can give you information about Colleen's perspective on project concerns or worries. Again, you do not have to agree or disagree. Just note the information, and if necessary for your own understanding of the concern, ask for additional clarifying information. For example, if Colleen says, "I'm concerned that the basic premise of this project might change if we add the Web Requisition software," you might follow up with a question like, "What worries you about the Web Requisition software?" Then you might learn, "The Web Requisition software changes this project from a centralized to a decentralized approach. That means a scope change, and the technical risks will be higher."

What else would you like me to know?

This question invites Colleen to tell you something important to her about which you might not have asked. It also reinforces that you are interested in what she has to say. She may not accept your invitation immediately, but leave the door open should she think of something later. The preceding questions may have caused Colleen to think about herself in relation to her project in new and different ways. Do not be surprised if she cannot think of anything in the moment.

What would you like to ask me?

This question invites Colleen to ask you questions. Until now she may have been so intent on answering your questions that she may not have had an opportunity to ask any questions of her own. Some people ask questions freely, but others need an invitation. Some people perceive that asking questions is a power dynamic. In other words, people who ask questions are sometimes perceived as being in a power position over people who answer questions. Some people who might otherwise feel one down in this situation may feel less so if they have an opportunity to ask questions of you.

Ask Open-ended Questions

A special set of three process questions is open-ended and provides an opening for a wide range of responses about lots of things, including energy. Use these questions when you need to be less direct, such as when taking over an existing project team or getting acquainted with a new project team member who has just joined your team. Because the questions are so open-ended, you will have to listen more carefully to pick out responses that relate to the person's energy.

What brings you to this project?

This is about the past. It can help you understand some of the events, circumstances, and motivations that led the person to be here, now on this project. You might be surprised to discover that a common acquaintance, event, or experience connects you both. Connection can be important in a collaborative working relationship. Share your own answer with the person if it seems appropriate. If you listen carefully, you might learn that the person came to this project because she was "excited to have an opportunity to use the tool set currently in use on this project." Now you know that she has energy for the tool set. Or you might learn that she came to this project because she "hated writing test plans" on her previous project. Now you know that she may have no energy for writing test plans. Other forms of this question are:

- How did you come to be here on this project?
- How do you happen to be on this project?

Be patient. Some people may not be used to this type of question. You might get a 15-minute personal history lesson. If you have the time, let the person talk. Given the opportunity, people generally talk about what is important to them. Or you might get a terse answer like, "My boss told me to show up here." You may want to follow up with a question like, "What was it like to be told to show up here?" Or you may want to move on to the next question.

What's it like being on this project?
This is about the present. It can help you understand thoughts and feelings that might not be expressed otherwise—both excitements and worries. Together you may discover a common worry or excitement that can be another point of connection. Share your own answer with the person if it seems appropriate. Responses can vary widely and can include:

- "It's cold in here. Guess I need to bring a sweater."
- "Everyone has been so welcoming."
- "I haven't found the restrooms yet."
- "Is it really true that we can't talk to the users?"
- "I am anxious to get started, but I don't have an assignment yet."

Listen carefully for clues to how this person is currently experiencing your project. Is it a good experience? Bad? Some of both? How could you make it better for this person? Where is this person's energy right now?

What would you like to have happen for yourself on this project?
This is about the future. Here is where you listen for clues about this person's goals, hopes, and wishes. This may be the most difficult question to answer. Many people have been socialized not to express their wants for themselves. Such people may need a little more time and encouragement to answer this question. You might get an answer like, "To be part of a successful project." I would want to follow this response up with a question like, "If this project is successful, what would you get for yourself as a result?" I think it really helps

free up energy for people to be able to consciously connect their wants with a successful project outcome.

"SEEING" ENERGY

People are often skeptical when I tell them I can "see" a person's energy. When I enter for the first time the physical space of a project team—their work environment—I can usually "see" their energy before anyone says a word. I am not referring to a *Kirlian aura* (discovered in 1939 by Semyon Kirlian). I have never seen such an aura around any person or any other living thing. I am very sensitive, though, to how people hold themselves, where they look with their eyes, how they move, what they do with their feet and hands, and whether their skin seems bright or pallid.

I am careful not to conclude anything from this type of observation. I might make a mental note, "Oh, that's interesting. This group seems very alive, energetic, and active." I become curious about where all their energy is coming from. Or my mental note might be, "Oh, that's interesting. This group seems very lethargic, drained of energy, and passive." I become curious about where all their energy went. In either case, I will ask some energy questions once I have made contact with the group.

LOOKING FOR PATTERNS IN RESPONSES

As you make contact with each person, listen carefully to their words and their voice, and watch their body language, including their breathing. Pay attention to what is said, and to what is not said. If you are observant, you can get clues about which questions to ask next. The worst thing you can do when trying to learn about a person is to judge his or her answers—that is, explain why he or she is wrong or misinformed. At this point, try to keep an open communication channel. Judging a person's answer is a sure way to close the channel.

As you talk with more team members, you may start to notice patterns emerging in their responses. By patterns, I mean a significant number of individuals freely commenting on (or avoiding) the same issue without solicitation. Here are a few examples of patterns I detected in a recent project review:

- Decisions do not seem to stick on this project.
- Many people seem concerned about knowledge transfer because the external implementation partner is leaving soon and the partner's employees have done most of the technical work.

- No one is talking about the transition from development to production operations. There is currently no production organization set up to accept this application.
- Almost everyone expressed a concern about lack of management oversight.

Further analysis was required to determine the specific impacts of these patterns on the project, but it was clear to me without much analysis that a significant amount of emotional energy was being spent on them—energy that could be used more productively.

Once in a while I run into a situation where the majority of people on a project team seem very resistant to answering my "energy" questions. They don't seem to want to talk to me about what's important to them. This too is a pattern that requires further analysis. There could be lots of reasons for this, some of which could be about the project, about me, or about neither. For example:

- Some people remember that the previous time a consultant visited, lots of people lost their jobs.
- Some people cannot acknowledge even to themselves that they hate working on their project.
- Some people really like their project, but don't want anyone to find out.
- Some people are aware that they hate their project, but are helpless to do anything about it.
- Some people believe that work should not be enjoyable—that's why they call it work.

USING WHAT YOU LEARN

Ultimately, you want to shape your team's work environment so that every individual is working as much as possible with his or her energy as opposed to against it. You can do that more effectively when you know what energizes each individual, and what team patterns are potentially draining your team's energy.

Knowing your team's patterns can enable you to do at least four things:

1. Name the patterns, thus bringing them to the conscious awareness of everyone involved without blaming any individual.
2. Explore the underlying issues.
3. Make specific recommendations of your own about how to address the underlying issues.
4. Ask the project team for ideas about how to address the underlying issues.

The awareness part is important because naming the pattern makes it more possible for everyone to talk about what is really going on in creative ways. The recommendations and ideas are important because they provide concrete ideas about what to do to move forward.

As a project leader, you may not always be able to perfectly match the available work with the available energy. That is reality. However, this reality should not prevent you from finding your team's energy. As project situations change, you may be able to recognize opportunities to improve the match.

To recap:

- A powerful project leader knows how to *find the energy* of the individuals on his project team. Then he attempts to create a work environment that maximizes the natural attraction between the available work and the available energy.
- Powerful project leaders do not resort to threat/reward tactics because they know how to create an environment that encourages employees' own natural motivation.
- To find your project team's energy, begin by making contact with the individuals on your team.
- Given the freedom and encouragement to do so—and if they feel safe enough—people will usually talk about what is important to them.
- To find the energy, you need to ask *energy* questions.
- A special set of three process questions provides an opening for a wide range of responses about lots of things, including energy. The three questions have variations in their forms. One form is:
  —What brings you to this project?
  —What is it like being on this project?
  —What would you like to have happen for yourself on this project?
- Ultimately, you want to shape your team's work environment so that every individual is working as much as possible with his or her energy as opposed to against it. You can do that more effectively when you know what energizes each individual, and what team patterns are potentially draining your team's energy.
- As a project leader, you may not always be able to perfectly match the available work with the available energy. That is reality.

Try this:

1. Try the signature exercise yourself. Ask someone to time you with your dominant hand first, then your nondominant hand. (No fair if you are

ambidextrous. If you are ambidextrous you do not have a dominant hand.)

2. Practice "seeing" energy. When you notice someone looking like he has low energy, check your perception with the person. Do not worry that you get it wrong sometimes. Recognize that the "seeing" part is not the conclusion. It is only an observation, which then needs to be checked out and verified.
3. Try the energy questions. Start with a project team member with whom you have a good relationship. See if you learn anything new about that person. Were there any surprises?

Chapter 11

BEING A HELPFUL PERSON

One of the ways a powerful project leader leads others is by being a helpful person. If she is truly helpful, a project leader may amplify her power to get things done by adding her power to the power of the people she helps. When this amplification occurs, the effects on herself and the people she helps may include higher self-esteem, more creativity, and greater productivity.

Perhaps you have known a leader whose team members just seemed to work better when she was around than when she wasn't. Maybe you did not notice specifically what she did; nevertheless, the effects were undeniable. When a project leader is truly helpful, people can act independently because the leader has let them know they are trusted. They do not need her constant approval because they feel good about themselves and their work. The leader shares her decision-making power with them, but is clear about which decisions they can make on their own, and which need her involvement.

If a project leader is not truly helpful, her power to get things done may be dampened and she may have a dampening effect on the power of the people she is attempting to help. The effects of this on herself and the people she is attempting to help may include lower self-esteem, restricted creativity, and impoverished productivity.

Perhaps you have known a leader whose team members seemed at odds with each other when she was around. Maybe it took forever to get anything done when that person was around. I have observed the negative effects of such leaders many times. People appear to be overly dependent on such leaders, always checking for permission before doing even trivial tasks. They seem to seek approval from the leader constantly. They are afraid to make decisions on their own because the leader does not share her decision-making power. I cannot say with scientific certainty that those leaders were the sole cause of the effects, but there appears to be a correlation.

Who should decide what is helpful? How does one become more helpful? What are some ways of helping? What makes help not helpful?

WHO SHOULD DECIDE WHAT IS HELPFUL?

I feel uncomfortable watching someone struggle or in apparent pain. My instinct is to jump in and help—unsolicited. I find it hard to resist my good intention. I see lots of people doing this. I interpret this to mean that other people, like me, feel uncomfortable, have a good intention, and jump in to help.

Often when I have jumped in, I have been perceived as not helpful—regardless of my good intention. I now refer to these unrestrained attempts of mine as *inflicting my help*. Naming it this way makes it easier for me to resist jumping in. I do not like to think I would *inflict* anything on anybody. I would guess that most of us have had help inflicted on us at least once during our lives. Perhaps it was a teacher, or a relative, or a friend. I do not know about you but, even when the inflicted "help" is actually helpful, I still feel put upon. I also feel somewhat disempowered. I may want help, but at the same time, I want to feel like I can do it myself.

When someone inflicts his help on me, the question of whether I can do it myself grows very large in my mind. When the inflicted help is *not* helpful, I feel put upon and angry. Not only do I get no help, but the attempt is very intrusive. For example, in a project team meeting, a teammate brings up a new problem FYI—just to make the team aware. As a project leader, I can unintentionally inflict help if I ignore the FYI and start telling the teammate how to fix the problem.

Who should decide what is helpful? I propose that it is the potential receiver—not the giver. Yes, the potential receiver decides:

- Whether he wants any help or not
- What would be helpful and when it would be helpful
- From whom to receive the help.

HOW DOES ONE BECOME MORE HELPFUL?

To be a helpful person who truly helps, you will need to develop the following abilities:

1. Practice good self-care.
2. Center yourself.

3. Make contact with the other person.
4. Find out if he or she wants any help.
5. Find out directly what would be helpful to the person.
6. Negotiate what you will do to give the help and what the other person will do to receive the help.
7. Determine how you will both know if the person was helped.

Ability 1—Practice Good Self-care

Put your oxygen mask on first. Airline flight attendants instruct us to put our oxygen masks on first before attempting to put a mask on a child. They tell us this for only one reason: *You cannot help a child or anyone else if you are unconscious.*

A helpful person always has at least one prerequisite obligation: sufficient self-care so as to continue to be strong enough to help others. This is not selfish, although some might perceive it that way. There is a difference between self-care and being selfish. Selfish means concerned primarily with one's own welfare regardless of others. Self-care means concerned with one's own welfare too, but not regardless of others. A helpful person practices good self-care so he is able to help himself and others.

When we give to ourselves with intention and compassion
we have so much more to give others.[1]

When we are well-provisioned in mind, body, and spirit, we are more able to give ourselves to help others. Some people believe giving to ourselves should be lowest on our priority list. To do otherwise would be selfish. I have known people who practiced this belief to the point of exhaustion and illness. They eventually got so depleted that they no longer had the strength or resources to help anyone, even themselves.

Self-care does not mean always putting yourself first either. The point is to provision yourself properly so that you maintain your ability to keep helping. Here are some examples of self-care provisions, the correct measure of which can only be determined by each individual:

- Sleep
- Healthy food
- Exercise
- Recreation

[1] Nyra Hill, personal e-mail, December 19, 2000.

- Solitude
- Financial stability
- Professional development
- Personal development
- Support system of family, friends, and colleagues.

Ability 2—Center Yourself

The martial art Aikido[2] provides a beautifully simple yet powerful model of helping: center, enter, turn. The Japanese words for these are *chushin*, *irimi*, *tenkan*, respectively. Chushin means center, especially the body, because you are more stable when your body is centered over your feet as opposed to leaning to one side or the other. A more expansive kind of centering would include mind, spirit, energy, vital force, and intention—all of which are sometimes referred to as Ki. When your mind and body are unified, this is called Shinshin Toitsu.[3]

There are many techniques for centering, including meditation, guided imagery, and breathing. Breathing is the simplest and most powerful. A few deep cleansing breaths can have a noticeable effect on your ability to relax, think, and feel. If you attempt to make contact with the other person (Ability 3) before you are centered, the result can be unpredictable, even unpleasant. An example of this would be trying to get someone to cooperate with you by blowing up and screaming at them.

Ability 3—Make Contact with the Other Person

Irimi, or enter, is a metaphor for making contact with the other person. Making contact means to make a connection. The connection can be physical, emotional, intellectual, or a combination of these. It can be very brief—for a microsecond or two—or for a longer period of time. Making contact is a way of saying, "I see you. I hear you. I am ready to receive and to give." If you do not make contact first, the quality of whatever happens next between you and the other person may fall short of what you expect.

Aikido thinks of most movement as being circular or spiraling. Irimi brings a person into the circle of movement, so that the energy of the person can be guided along the circular plane—much like catching a Frisbee on your finger. You let the circular energy spin around your finger. Then you send it on its way in the same or an alternate direction

---

[2]Eric Sotnak, http://home.neo.lrun.com/sotnak/primer.html.

[3]Kjartan Clausen, http://www.aikidofaq.com/dictionary/misc.html.

with a minimum of effort.[4] Irimi is always done in a respectful manner—with positive intention and genuine care for self and other.

Ability 4—Find Out If He or She Wants Any Help

This relates closely to making contact with the other person. Before you start helping, find out if the person wants any help. For example, some individuals have a strong resistance to receiving help even when they want it. The help these individuals may need is *help with receiving help*.

As a project leader, you have to be watchful that your project does not suffer because someone cannot accept help. If you practice good self-care, you may not be devastated by an answer like, "No. Thank you. I do not want any help right now." If your need to help is greater than the other person's desire for help, an answer like that could be difficult for you to accept.

Ability 5—Find Out Directly What Would Be Helpful to the Person

This is part of tenkan—turning movement. Once you have entered respectfully with the person and determined that he wants help, you can begin moving with the person's energy. You move with a person's energy first by finding out what would be helpful to him. After you have determined what would be helpful, you then have a direction toward which to move with him. Do not attempt to move with someone without first centering, then making contact.

Ability 6—Negotiate What You Will Do to Give the Help and What the Other Person Will Do to Receive the Help

This is also part of tenkan. It is not enough to know what would be helpful. Together you and the other person may want to clarify what you will do and what he will do. The negotiation is important because you may not be the person who will directly provide the help. Your role might be to suggest names of other people who could provide the help or to provide contact information or coaching on how to best use the help. The person receiving the help will have some responsibilities. It is important to clarify those too.

Ability 7—Determine How You Will Both Know If the Person Was Helped

This will complete one cycle of tenkan with the person. It also makes an opening for another cycle. Part of your negotiation with

---

[4] Kjartan Clausen, http://www.aikidofaq.com/principles.html/#22.

the other person might include some kind of feedback mechanism. The feedback mechanism provides a way of knowing if the person was actually helped, and both the giver and the receiver can have a sense of closure.

WHAT ARE SOME WAYS OF HELPING?

If you have only one way of helping and you use it in every situation, sometimes it may work and other times it may not. It's better to have several ways of helping in your tool kit and to pick the most appropriate one for the situation.

In Greek mythology, the gods would sometimes punish mortals by granting them their prayers. If I give someone the help he asks for when I know the help may be harmful in the long term, am I being truly helpful? I think not. The *center, enter, turn* principle provides a disciplined approach to helping that may avoid that dilemma. The discipline of the approach provides opportunities to check yourself first so that you enter balanced, connect with the person respectfully, find out what would be helpful and not helpful, agree on who is going to do what, and learn what the result was.

Here are several specific ways of helping I currently have in my tool kit. Feel free to add them to yours.

Witnessing

Helping does not always need to involve speaking, moving, or touching a person. Sometimes the help I want is to have someone I trust sit near me without speaking or touching me. The physical presence alone of another human being I trust is comforting to me. Sometimes a light touch on my shoulder, back, arm, or hand adds comfort, and sometimes not. One picture of this is me silently sitting with my struggle and a friend silently sitting next me. That may be all I need.

Other times I may want to express my struggle with my voice. I may want my friend sitting next to me to just listen and not comment. Just saying my struggle so my friend can hear me gives me some measure of satisfaction. Doing so makes my struggle seem more real and not quite so large as it appears in my mind. Saying it helps me know that my struggle is not just in my head. I appreciate receiving this kind help in certain situations, and I like giving this kind of help when it fits.

These are ways I like to be witnessed. As a project leader, understanding how you like to be witnessed can help sensitize you to how others might like to be witnessed. But, you cannot know for certain how others like to be witnessed, so you need to check it out.

In a project setting, imagine that your project was just audited. One of your young, inexperienced developers got hammered pretty hard even though overall the project passed. He is sitting in his cubicle head down, fighting back his tears. Everyone else has gone home. He notices you and invites you in.

One way you could witness for him is to just pull up a chair beside his and sit quietly. Do not say anything until he speaks. When he gives you an opening, simply ask him if there is anything you can do that would be helpful to him. If no opening seems forthcoming, you can say, "May I ask you a question?" If he indicates in the affirmative, then you can ask him if there is anything you can do that would be helpful to him. If he responds in the negative, then continue sitting quietly. Remember, it may enough that you are there. It is not always necessary for words to be exchanged.

When you have to leave, quietly get up and leave. If he asks, you can explain that you have to leave now and that you will check with him first thing tomorrow (or whatever realistically fits for you.)

Nurturing

This kind of help feels to me like a big, soft, fluffy pillow. I give this kind of help when I want to reassure someone that he is competent and acceptable, and especially when he makes mistakes. This kind of help is gentle, focused on the positive, and connects through our hearts. It conveys a message like, "I see you. I hear you. I am with you. You are just fine the way you are." This kind of help is never critical or punishing. I like giving and receiving this kind of help when it fits.

Some people might be afraid this kind of help will make others too soft. Maybe you recognize this message, "How will you ever learn anything if I am too soft on you?" I appreciate that fear. Perhaps the fear comes from not knowing how much to give or when to give it. That would make sense if I am one for whom nurturing has been out of balance in my life—either not enough or too much relative to other kinds of help.

Personally, I think the world could use a lot more nurturing. However, I would not want nurturing to be the only way of helping in my tool kit. In a project setting, this way of helping may be appropriate when you are mentoring someone, grooming him or her for a future key position.

Just Doing It

Occasionally the helpee wants his helper to just do it for him, like when he is feeling weak or unsure, or when time is critical. For example, as my own project leader, I cannot afford the time to take a course in Japanese so I can be sure that I am using the words *chushin*, *irimi*, and *tenkan* accurately in this chapter. I have colleagues whom I can call upon for help with this. In this case, my colleague Jiro Fujita, who is Japanese, checked my work for accuracy and told me what I needed to change. One of the tradeoffs with this kind of help is deeper learning. Some day I might want to deepen my knowledge of the Japanese language. For now I will settle for saving some time and learning only a few words.

In a project setting, this way of helping may be appropriate when someone occasionally gets overwhelmed with backlogged work. If you are able, you may offer to do some of the work yourself or to offload it in some other way.

Doing Nothing

This way of helping is sometimes the best choice when you are not sure what to do. Or when you don't feel competent to do what has been asked of you. You honor the person you are trying to help by telling her your truth.

For example, you might say to Ginny, "Ginny, I am not sure what to do." Ginny may respond with a specific request. If you really want to help Ginny, but do not think you are competent to fulfill her request, you might say something like, "Ginny, I am sorry. I do not know how to do what you asking. I wish I did." Saying this can be difficult, especially when you really want to help. However, it can be risky to help when you do not know what you are doing.

Giving Feedback

Feedback is tricky. Most of the time, I think people want feedback—especially when they are feeling strong and are able to hear it without being flattened. Feedback can be immensely helpful, even though it is not always easy to hear. But sometimes people are not strong enough to receive this kind of help. They might need a small dose of nurturing before and after the feedback. Because I know this is true about myself, I am very careful when others ask me for feedback to remember: center, enter, and turn.

In a project setting, this way of helping may be appropriate when you have information from your own observations that may be helpful or useful to someone. Be sure to check first to see if the person is ready to receive the feedback. In rare cases, as a project leader you may feel you need to give someone feedback whether he or she wants it or not.

For example, you may be putting someone on a formal performance improvement plan as part of their due process prior to possible termination. Even in this extreme case, you can say something like, "Anne, I have some feedback for you. It might be difficult or painful to hear, but I am obligated to give it to you. Is there anything you need right now to help you receive it?"

Sharing Expertise

Sharing your expertise with someone is a powerful way to help. When you share your expertise, you magnify your influence in your project and in the world. A piece of you gets passed on to another person. That person may take your gift, make it their own, and then pass it on to yet another person. There may or may not be any visible credit, citation, or reference to you. But do not let that stop you from giving this kind of help.

Each year I give away some of my expertise without charging for it. I feel good inside when I do that. I am fascinated by the many stories of how my help moved through the community. The stories find their way back to me—sometimes years later.

WHAT MAKES HELP NOT HELPFUL?

I have my tongue in my cheek a bit here. Here are some rules to live by if you want to go around inflicting your unhelp on others. If any of these seem familiar, please do not be too tough on yourself. By the way, I have mastered each one of these rules myself. Presently, I try not to live by these, although I do slip occasionally.

1. Always help without asking or being asked.
2. Always try to protect everyone from struggle and pain. This responsibility has been given to you by a higher power.
3. Never ask the other person what would be helpful to her. She won't know. You should always read her mind or just know what would be helpful to her. Besides, if she knew what would be helpful, she would do it herself.
4. Always know what the other person is feeling without asking him. After all, you have feelings too. You are an empathetic person. So the other person must be feeling the same things you are feeling.
5. Everybody always needs your help. You have no choice but to give it. You need to be a helpful person. If you see a person who obviously needs help, jump in and help. Never mind if some people get offended when you help them. They're just fooling themselves if they think they don't need your help. Besides, it's still help even if the other person doesn't want it.

6. Never allow someone to help himself. He might figure out he doesn't need you. Always do it for him so he becomes dependent on you.
7. Never just sit and listen to someone. You must always take action and tell the person what to do. Better yet, do it for him. What a waste to just sit there like a bump on a log!
8. Always keep score so you know how many favors people owe you. The more favors people owe you, the more puffed up and important you can feel.
9. Always do something even when you don't know what you are doing. You might make the situation worse, but that is far better than admitting that you don't know how to help.

To recap:

- A powerful project leader is (among other things) a helpful person. If she is truly helpful, the effects on herself and the people she helps may include higher self-esteem, more creativity, and greater productivity.
- The potential receiver of help gets to decide:
  —Whether he wants any help or not
  —What would be helpful and when it would be helpful
  —From whom to receive the help.
- To be a helpful person who truly helps, you will need to develop the following abilities:
  —Practice good self-care
  —Center yourself
  —Make contact with the person
  —Find out if he or she wants any help
  —Find out directly what would be helpful to the person
  —Negotiate what you will do to give the help and what the other person will do to receive the help
  —Determine how you will both know if the person was helped.
- If you only have one way of helping and you use it all the time, sometimes it may work and other times it may not. It's better to have several ways of helping in your tool kit and to pick the most appropriate one for the situation.
- Sometimes, despite our best intentions, our help is not very helpful. There are lots of ways this can happen. One way is by attempting to help someone who has not asked for help.

Try this:

1. Have a discussion with a friend or trusted colleague using the following questions as a guide:
   —What did you learn about self-care growing up in your family?
   —What is easy about self-care for you?
   —What is difficult about self-care for you?
   —What did you learn about giving and receiving help growing up in your family?
   —Which is easier for you, giving help or receiving help?
   —What ways of helping do you have in your tool kit?

Variation: Write the answers to the same questions in your personal journal.

Part Three
SHAPING YOUR PROJECT'S CONTEXT

Your project always operates within a context. The context influences your project, and in turn, your project influences its context—in an ongoing cycle of change. It may be obvious that the context influences your project. Project leaders have always had to deal with this fact. Perhaps less obvious is that your project also influences its context. This is powerful knowledge because it empowers you to enter the cycle of change to intentionally shape the context in a way that your project benefits. For example, information is very much a part of your project's context. One way to shape your project's context so that your project benefits is by increasing the amount of useful information that flows into, through, and out of your project.

Here is how such influencing might work. Let's say your project's context includes:

- A scope—information about the boundaries of the project's work
- A budget—information about the money available to spend
- Work planning assumptions—information about number of staff, estimation rules, and standard tools and methods
- A schedule—information about when the work should be accomplished.

Let's assume that these four elements of your project's context seem reasonable and useful to start with. As time passes, though, you notice that some of the elements have changed in the following ways:

- The scope has expanded.
- The budget has remained the same.

- A few of your most skilled and experienced staff have been assigned to other projects, leaving them working only half-time on your project. The rest are less experienced, which further drains your experienced staff because they have to "help" the less experienced staff.
- The standard tools are immature and your staff spends a lot of time working with the tool vendor's technical support people.
- The estimation rules do not seem to apply to the kind of work your team is doing.
- The schedule has not changed.

Your project is now being shaped differently—perhaps negatively—as a result of these changes in its context. You and your team are expected to do more work with fewer resources using immature tools, and do it all on the same schedule—which was probably unrealistic anyway because of the mismatched estimation rules. As project leader, what do you do? You can:

- Accept this context as unchangeable, put your head down, and keep charging.
- Whine and complain a lot to your boss.
- Tell your staff to work smarter.
- Get some useful factual information about how your project is being shaped (i.e., affected) by the changes in its context. Use that information to present a strong case (i.e., give useful information) to your boss for changing your project's context so that it shapes your project more positively.

For example, you might recommend reestimating the work based on actual experience to date, modifying the schedule to bring it more in line with the new estimates and revised scope, or adding staff to bring your team up to the appropriate full-time equivalent level. It may be difficult for your boss to hear your recommendations, but it will be more difficult for her to ignore the information when it is factual, truthful, and documented. Perhaps with this useful information, your boss will be able to see that unless changes are made, the project may be headed for serious trouble.

Chapter 12
GETTING USEFUL INFORMATION

If you are the project leader, people on your team may look to you for information in the form of decisions, advice, recommendations, and support. People outside your team may look to you for information in the form of status reports, progress reports, problem resolution, and deliverables. All these forms of information—decisions, advice, recommendations, support, status, progress reports, problem resolution, and deliverables—are as useful as the information you use to create them.

Project leaders may assume that getting information is elementary, even ancillary to their real project work. They may believe that they have no control over which information is useful and which is not. They may passively accept a mixed bag of both kinds. Because these project leaders underestimate their ability to actively get useful information, their projects may not be as successful as they could be. Projects whose leaders give a high priority to getting useful information will run more smoothly because less time is wasted correcting mistakes, clearing up misrepresentations and misunderstandings, unclogging communication jams, and rebuilding lost trust.

Information is to powerful project leadership as air is to breathing. When I breathe in air my body seems to work better, especially if the air is clean and pollutant-free. When a project leader gets information, he can be a more powerful advocate, advisor, and decision-maker for his project, especially if the information is useful. Thus, the ability to get useful information is a very important skill for a project leader.

WHAT MAKES INFORMATION USEFUL?

What makes information useful to a project leader can be as different as any two people can be. But there can also be a lot of commonality. For me, project information is useful when it furthers my understanding of my project's:

- Current situation
- Progress over time
- Necessary course corrections.

I want the right information, and in a consistent form. I would rather not have to continually clarify the context of, verify, translate, or convert the information. Here are some examples of what I mean:

- I like to see *signature sign-off sheets for major deliverables* such as project work plans, budgets, requirements documents, and so on that indicate the date of each signature. That way I can tell how long the signature cycle takes. Without dates I do not know if the signature cycle took two days or two weeks. I cannot know if a document was signed prior to or after a significant change to the document. I like to see a written definition of what a signature on a document means.
- I like to see a *common status report format*. Each status item should be referenced to a work breakdown structure (WBS) or task number on the work plan. Without this reference, it is difficult to tie status items back to the work plan tasks. The author's name and contact information should also appear on the status report in case I want to ask for additional information. The word "complete" should have a consistent meaning. In some cases a task can be noted as complete because the work was done, yet it may not have been verified as acceptable to users.
- I like to see *deliverables added to work plans* that are task- or activity-based. A deliverable is a concrete, identifiable outcome or a finished product such as a document, a piece of hardware, a test report, or a ready test environment. Deliverables give you a clearer sense of progress. Tasks tell you that something is being worked on; a deliverable tells you that something is finished and delivered.

To get useful information, I accept my responsibility to create the necessary feedback loops and quality checks, and to be vigilant about using them. I accept that, as a project leader, I may have to teach others how to make information more useful to me. I do not expect people to learn this by reading my mind. My teaching may have to be repeated often, and still there will be times when I will have to go back to the source to clarify the context of, verify, translate, or convert some information.

When I am hired to review a project in trouble, I almost always find an opportunity to teach project leaders some ways to get more useful information. These leaders often seemed surprised by how low-tech, familiar, and maybe even obvious some of my recommendations seem. When anyone says of my recommendations, "Oh, we already know to do that," I simply ask them to show me some examples. Sometimes they can. Usually they cannot. I also make a special effort to express my appreciation to any leaders who actually do what they know they should do.

Here are several means of getting more useful information that seem to be effective:

Age—Make sure that all information is dated. Include the creation date and the revision date. It is much easier to determine the age of the information when information is dated this way. This is especially important when you want to see only the most current information. Dating information this way also makes it possible to track how information has changed over time if it becomes necessary to do that. If you use project management software that can automatically time-stamp information when it is updated and printed, be sure that you have that feature turned on.

Consistent format and language—Ask that information be put into a consistent format and language. If you get information from several different teams, provide them with a template for each type of information they give you. Each template can specify the layout of information, define terms, and provide examples. Status reports, issue logs, charts, and other pieces of project information are easier to compare across individuals and teams when consistent formats and terms are used to produce them. There are no right or wrong templates—only more or less useful ones.

A reasonable goal would be to make the information you receive more useful while not creating an oppressive burden on the people providing the information. Often this can be a matter of standardizing and clarifying terms, not necessarily requiring more information. When people do not know what you want, they sometimes give you more information than necessary to cover the bases. In these cases, less information can sometimes be better than more. Terms such as "open," "pending," "closed," "priority," "start date," "status," "deliverable," and "milestone" will be more useful if they mean the same to everyone using them on your project.

Vagueness—Avoid vague, sweeping, general statements without factual details. For example, a statement like "The team is working hard to finish on time" is a cliché. While the intent may be to reassure the reader, the statement is superficial and does not further anyone's understanding of the project's current situation, progress, or necessary course corrections.

What does "working hard" mean? Would anyone say that the team is not working hard? Which work was finished? What does "on time" mean? A more useful statement would be something like, "The team completed 14 test scripts this week against a scheduled 10 scripts. Four of the 14 completed scripts had slipped in previous weeks. All test scripts scheduled to date have now been completed. Each team member worked four hours overtime this week to complete the 14 test scripts."

Charts and diagrams—If you take information from planning charts and diagrams—Gantt, Program Evaluation and Review Technique (PERT), Critical Path Analysis—insist that the charts contain a legend and a key. The legend should explain any symbols used on the chart. The key should explain any terms, acronyms, and abbreviations used on the chart. You should be able to look down the timeline on a Gantt chart and quickly spot which tasks and major milestones are completed and which are slipping. Each major milestone should have a corresponding deliverable. The resulting deliverable for each major milestone should be annotated on the chart. You may sometimes want to examine a deliverable, like when you want more detailed information than is available from the chart or diagram alone.

For example, let's say that a major milestone is *detailed designs complete*, and the deliverable is *detailed design documents*. If the chart shows that this milestone is completed, you may want to randomly check some of the design documents to make sure that they have the proper approval signatures and they conform to any standards in use.

Work plans—Work plans that specify which work is to be accomplished are very useful. But people sometimes read more into work plans than is actually written there. When this happens, misunderstanding is not far behind. Specify both which work is and *is not* going to be accomplished. This helps the boundaries of the work come into clearer view, minimizing the likelihood of misunderstandings about boundaries.

Authorized signatures—Insist on authorized signatures for key working documents such as work plans, staffing plans, test plans, designs, and requirements. When such documents are revised, make sure that authorized signatures are reobtained for the revision. People usually (but not always) read more carefully documents they sign. When people do read more carefully before signing, the information communicated in these documents is more likely to be useful. Unfortunately there is little protection from people who sign documents without knowing what they are signing, and then later recant because they claim they did not know what they were signing.

Author contact information—Insist that all project documents contain author contact information: name, location, telephone, email. Occasionally I want to contact the author of a project document to get more detail or to clarify something I read. If I am doing this as a prerequisite to deciding how useful the information is to me, not having the contact information may significantly delay my decision. Such a delay could render time-sensitive information useless.

Problem statement—Frequently I receive documents that state a solution or solution method without stating the problem to be solved. These documents are often accompanied by a request for feedback such as, "What do you think of my solution or solution method?" My stock response to such requests is, "This looks like it could be a wonderful solution! However, I cannot be sure since I do not know which problem it is intended to solve." People who like to jump to a solution before they understand a problem often get upset with me when I respond that way. I guess we all jump sometimes; I know I do. Nevertheless, I do not know how to evaluate my solution or anyone else's without knowing what problem it is intended to solve.

Activity vs. progress—Many project status reports contain statements of activity but no statements about progress toward project deliverables. Here are a few examples of what I mean from a weekly status report:

- "I attended the Jolly Jalapeno project meeting."
- "I worked on that security bug we discovered Sunday morning."
- "Granger team is working on moving ourselves to the new building."
- "Programming and unit testing continue."

This kind of information can be made more useful by adding some indication of what has been accomplished—specifically, concrete progress toward a deliverable. That might look something like this:

- "I attended the Jolly Jalapeno project meeting. The standard development environment decision was made. This means we can officially start coding our work packages next Monday. Waiting for that decision has put us one week behind schedule."
- "I worked on that security glitch we discovered Sunday morning. The vendor's technical support said a fix will be in the next release, due out in two weeks. He was able to provide a workaround until then. I am testing the workaround now and plan to put it into production this weekend. No customer data can be affected by the glitch. This will not hold up the production rehearsal milestone next week."

- "Granger team is working on moving ourselves to the new building. The date of the move is not settled, but most likely it will be the first of August, after the LAN is connected and the general ledger upgrade development work is completed. Issues remaining to be resolved are: installing printers and copiers, delivering storage cabinets for supplies, and repairing several toilets that do not work properly. Work orders have been completed, signed, and scheduled for all these issues."
- "Programming and unit testing continue. Our target this week was 393 work units coded, reviewed, unit-tested, and approved. To date, 375 are coded and reviewed, and 316 are unit-tested and approved. This shortfall can be attributed to a recurring test environment hardware issue (now resolved) and Zebra building LAN problems (see issues). Progress chart is attached."

Interpretations—Sometimes factual information comes to you embellished by the sender's interpretations. The sender may be completely unaware of the embellishment. It is human nature for us to interpret what we observe; we often do it automatically without thinking about it. I have to make a conscious effort not to do it. The problem arises when one cannot tell which is the factual information and which is interpretation. Here is an example of what I mean:

"The go/no-go decision was made today. The decision is to delay go-live for two weeks. The delay reflects poorly on the team because we will miss our go-live milestone date."

The factual information in this statement is: "The go/no-go decision was made today" and "The decision is to delay go-live for two weeks." The interpretation part is: "reflects poorly on the team because we will miss our go-live date." There can be other interpretations of the delay. One such interpretation is that the team is very wise not to proceed with go-live if the risk it too high.

Interpretations provide information too. But they provide information about the writer and not necessarily about the facts. If an interpretation is not labeled as such, the reader might take it as a fact. Encourage people who give you information to omit their interpretations, or if that is too difficult, to at least identify what is fact and what is interpretation.

Context—It is difficult to evaluate information without its context. For example, one January afternoon I received an email from Jessica, whom I did not know. I recognized the "@" part of her email address as that of a client. Jessica's message was short and to the point. It said, "Please provide your Tax ID number. Thank you." There was no context with this message. I could have guessed that since it was January it might have had something to do with 1099 tax information. I was annoyed. I was not about to give my Tax ID number to someone I do not know just because she asked for it. So I replied to her email and said, "Jessica, who are you? And why are you asking me for my Tax ID number?" A few days later she came back with the context that was missing from her first email. She explained that she was a representative of my client. She said she needed my Tax ID to prepare a 1099 tax form. I thanked her for the explanation, and reminded her that since I was incorporated I did not believe a 1099 tax form was necessary. I never heard from Jessica again.

Ask people who give you information to package it with its context. In this example, context includes purpose (prepare a 1099), place (location of my client), time (tax time), roles (her—representative of the client company, probably accounting, me—consultant), conditions (legal requirement to mail 1099s to recipients by January 31), and objects (Tax ID number, 1099 form).

WHAT KIND OF INFORMATION IS USEFUL?

Each project leader will have her own ideas about what kind of information is useful. The specifics may change from hour to hour depending on where her attention is focused. For a project leader to be a powerful advocate, advisor, and decision-maker for her project, she must be able to get useful information on an ongoing basis from each of the following general categories: management, technical, customer, and human systems.

Management information includes inputs to and outputs from project planning, project tracking and control, vendor contracting and management, production operations management, and ongoing maintenance and support management. With this information, management and project sponsors will be able to know if satisfactory progress is being made toward achieving their desired outcomes. Examples of information in this category could include: project plans, progress reports, corrective action logs, supplier and vendor communications, status reports, staffing reports, and budgets.

Technical information includes information about the technical skills, experience, and capabilities of the technical staff. It also includes technology architecture information such as hardware platforms, operating systems, programming languages, database management, user desktop requirements, and network design for performance. Examples of information in this category could include: design documents, code, test scripts, architecture documents, infrastructure diagrams, hardware topologies, performance targets and statistics, reliability data, configuration management data, and network and wiring diagrams.

Customer information includes information about project sponsorship, business requirements, user readiness, and user acceptance. Examples of information in this category could include: requirements compliance and traceability documents, business process flow diagrams, usability test results, training plans, training classes and materials, user acceptance certificates, and sponsor roles and responsibilities.

Human systems information includes information about the triumphs and troubles of human beings trying to work together in a social system like a project. Examples of information in this category could include: overt expressions of healthy and unhealthy working relationships, individuals' appropriate or inappropriate behavior in coping with their stress and upsets, circulation of rumors and other gossip, and verbal or written expressions of appreciation, complaints, hopes, wishes, puzzles, and joys.

REMEMBER SAFETY

People are generally more open and generous in giving information, especially about themselves, when they feel safe. Like useful information, feeling safe varies from individual to individual. However, people generally feel safer giving information when they:

- Know the purpose of your inquiry
- Understand the context of your questions
- Know how you intend to use the information they give
- Have choices about when, where, and how to respond
- Know that there are no right or wrong answers to your questions.

TYPES OF QUESTIONS TO ASK

Certain types of questions facilitate your ability to get useful information. You may use different types in the same conversation. For example, you may start with an *open question* to encourage a person to tell you whatever is on his mind. When you hear something you want to pursue further, you can use *furthering questions*. When you want a yes or no answer, use a *closed question*. You may want to know what the person thinks about the questions you are asking—*meta questions* are questions about questions. Periodically, you may want to check with the person to see if he is willing to continue. For that, use a *question that tests for willingness to continue*.

Here are some examples of these types of questions that may help you in getting useful information:

Open questions—Use an open question when you are interested in hearing whatever the person has to say. For example, "What do think is working well on your project?" If you want to focus the question a bit more you could ask, "What concerns do you have about the new test environment?"

Closed questions—Use a closed question when you want a more concise answer. For example, "Is it all right with you if we talk about the new test environment now?" or "How many work packages have been unit-tested?"

Meta questions—Use a meta question when you want to ask about the questions you are asking. For example, "Who else could answer this question?" "What have I not asked that you thought I would?" "Do my questions make sense?" "Are my questions helpful?" "Is there anything you want to ask me?" "Are you the right person to answer this question?"

Furthering questions—Use a furthering question when you want to go further with an answer to an earlier question. Here is an example of a dialogue between a consultant and a project director. The consultant is trying to understand what happened to cause the failure of a major component's implementation. Key to the failure was one of four project managers who went off on his own and would not collaborate with other project managers whose components were interdependent with his. Without the use of furthering questions, the consultant might not have learned all that the project director did to try to solve the problem. Not that the project director would have withheld, but it might not have occurred to him to go that far with his answers. He simply had not had any reason to believe anyone cared what he did. The dialogue contains several furthering questions.

Consultant: "Earlier you said that one of your project managers was operating in a vacuum." *(Furthering question)*: "Can you say more about that—what did you do?"

Project director: "I talked with him about it and asked him to share information with the other project managers. He did not comply with my request."

Consultant: *(Furthering question)*: "What did you do then?"

Project director: "I spoke to his functional manager, but she did not do anything about it."

Consultant: *(Furthering question)*: "Then what did you do?"

Project director: "I discussed the matter with the two executive sponsors. I guess they didn't think it was serious enough to be on their radar screen. Maybe I didn't make my case strong enough. They said it sounded like a personality clash and that I should work it out."

Consultant: *(Furthering question)*: "What did you do after you exhausted all apparent avenues of support?"

Project director: "I did what I usually do in this kind of situation—I just sucked it up and did the best I could knowing something bad was going to happen."

Questions that test for willingness to continue—Use this type of question when you want to check to see if the person is willing to continue. Being on the receiving end of questions can be tiring and stressful. It is a good idea to use this test at least every 15 minutes (sooner if you notice that the person seems distracted). For example, "I have been asking a lot of questions. How are you with receiving so many questions?" The quality of the information you get can be affected by the person's willingness to continue. Better to stop and try to reschedule the discussion if you suspect that the person's willingness is dropping off.

WAYS OF ASKING FOR INFORMATION

Begin by preparing yourself. Use these five safety-setting ideas to prepare yourself to ask for information. Review:

- How you will present the purpose of your inquiry
- How you will explain the context of your questions
- What you will say about how you intend to use the information
- What choices you will offer about when, where, and how to respond
- How you will give your assurance that there are no right or wrong answers to your questions.

Next, make a list of the information you want to get and formulate questions designed to get that information. Be as specific as you can. For example, your list might include: *status of the general ledger team's move to the new building*. The clearer you can be about what you mean by *status* in your question, the better. Test this by asking yourself, "How many ways could this question be answered? Which ones would satisfy me? For example, would you be satisfied if the answer was "working on it"? Use your answers as feedback to modify your questions.

Of course, there is always a chance that you will get an answer that you did not anticipate. Sometimes that can be a good thing—something surprisingly useful.

Next, consider the types of questions that might give you more useful information: open, closed, meta, furthering, and questions that test for willingness to proceed. Next, consider who could best give you the information you want. Make a list of the names of individuals from whom you want to get information.

After preparing yourself, make respectful contact with each person on your list. Ask for some of his time either now or later to talk about the information you are seeking. Be sure to communicate the safety-setting information. If you both agree to talk later, settle on a date and time. Appreciate him for being willing to give you the time and the information.

I do not recommend doing this with email. Face-to-face is my first choice, followed by telephone. If you decide to use email anyway, please remember to make respectful contact, ask for the person's time, and communicate the safety-setting information just as you would if you were face-to-face or on the telephone.

To recap:

- Information is to powerful project leadership as air is to breathing. When a project leader gets useful information, he can be a more powerful advocate, advisor, and decision-maker for his project.
- One way to positively shape your project's context is by increasing the amount of useful information that flows into, through, and out of your project.
- A project leader may have to teach others more than once how to make information more useful to him.
- For a project leader to be a powerful advocate, advisor, and decision-maker for her project, she must be able to get useful information on an ongoing basis from each of the following general categories: management information, technical information, customer information, and human systems information.
- People generally feel safer giving information when they:
  —Know the purpose of your inquiry
  —Understand the context of your questions
  —Know how you intend to use the information they give
  —Have choices about when, where, and how to respond
  —Know that there are no right or wrong answers to your questions.
- It is helpful to know several types of questions that you can use to get more useful information, such as: open questions, closed questions, meta questions, furthering questions, and questions that test for willingness to continue.
- The information you get will be more useful if your inquiry is thoughtfully planned and executed. Prepare yourself by carefully considering: how you will create safety, what information you are seeking, whom you will ask, what types of questions you will use, and how you will make respectful contact with those who will receive your questions.

Try this:

1. Use this brown-bag lunch topic: What would you like to teach others about what makes information more useful to you?
2. Alternate brown-bag lunch topic: What are your information pet peeves?
3. What other types of questions do you use to get the information you want?
4. What makes it safer for you to give information to others?

Chapter 13
GIVING USEFUL INFORMATION

As with getting useful information, you can also be a more powerful advocate, advisor, and decision-maker for your project when you give useful information. The ability to give useful information is very important to you as a project leader because people inside and outside your project team want and need information from you. They want it for their own purposes. You want them to have it so that they are better able to advocate for your project and give you the support you need. If the information you give them is not useful, they may start tuning you out. Eventually, you may lose important advocates for your project.

As we have seen, you, the project leader, determine the meaning of *useful information*. When getting information, you alone decide which information is useful to you and which is not. The meaning of *useful information* is very different, however, when you are giving information. In that situation, useful information means that:

- It is useful to the receiver—the person to whom you are giving the information
- It has the potential to shape your project's context in a positive way.

Eight practical techniques can help you increase your ability to give this kind of useful information.

TECHNIQUE 1: CONSIDER WHOM YOU WANT TO RECEIVE YOUR INFORMATION

What is useful to one receiver may not be useful to another. How can you know what will be useful to your receiver? Here are some possibilities:

- You can guess what would be useful.
- You can try to imagine what would be useful if you were in the other person's shoes.
- You can find out directly by asking the receiver what would be useful.
- If you cannot find out directly, you can state your intention to be helpful, and include that along with the information you provide.
- If you cannot find out directly, you can construct an opening for the receiver to tell you what is useful, and include that along with the information you provide.
- You can ask for acknowledgment of receipt so you at least know that the information was received. This closes the loop between you and receiver.

Let's look at an example.

Jack is a project leader who is taking over the Sizzling Serrano project. The previous project leader had to leave for health reasons. Alice, the project office director, wants to be helpful to Jack. She thanks him for accepting the project leadership. She is forwarding him some historical information about the project. She did not have an opportunity to speak with Jack prior to sending her message about what information would be helpful. Along with providing the historical information, she states her intention to be helpful, and leaves the door open for Jack to tell her directly what would be useful to him. She asks for acknowledgment that Jack received the information to close the loop. She thanks him in advance for his reply.

> Jack,
>
> Thank you for accepting the challenges and opportunities of leading the Sizzling Serrano project. I am enclosing the project initiation documents. You may find these useful as you take over this project. The documents will give you information about what happened before you arrived. My intention is to be helpful, so please let me know what would be most useful to you. I will be happy to provide whatever I can. Jack, please give me a short reply so I know you received this information. Thanks.
>
> Alice

The Sizzling Serrano project initiation documents may or may not be useful to Jack. If they are not, the invitation is there for Jack to let Alice know what would be useful.

TECHNIQUE 2: CONSIDER THE BURDEN OF PERFECTION

Forgive yourself in advance for not always being perfectly understood by your audience—those people to whom you are trying to give useful information. Also be aware that the unrelenting pursuit of perfection can be a terrible burden. It can delay or prevent us from giving any information at all for fear that the information, the delivery, or the interpretation of our information might be flawed in some way. If you resonate with this burden, then you are not alone in the world.

For others of us, the burden of perfection can be quite different. We know we are right, and it is our duty to set the world straight. It can be an awful burden to always know you are right. The rest of the world may not know how to receive so much rightness. If you resonate with this burden, then you are not alone in the world.

Whether your burden is knowing you are right, fearing you might not be, or somewhere in between, try to increase your awareness of how your burden helps or hinders you in giving useful information to others. I'm not suggesting that you change anything—like throwing off your burden. Change may come later if and when it fits for you. The first step is awareness. When you can, be aware of your burden as you construct your information and the delivery of your information.

TECHNIQUE 3: USE YOUR AWARENESS OF YOUR RESPONSE FILTERS

Your response filters can cause your outward behavioral response—giving information—to be different from your inside response (for more on response filters, see Chapter 3). This may lead to more or less useful information.

When I was contracted to review a project in trouble, my client, Derrick, did not understand why I wanted to explore how the project came to be in its current condition. Derrick just wanted to know "what do I do now?" and was dubious about what project history had to do with that. I felt impatient and frustrated with Derrick when I perceived that he did not want to deal with the project's history. In my mind I was shouting, "You just don't get it, do you! You better find someone else to help you, because I don't think I can!" That was my inside response–that is, no one, especially Derrick, could have heard me say that because it was inside my head. Said out loud, that response would not have been useful to Derrick–or myself. It would not have helped him "get it." He might have felt punished and become defensive. I might have lost a client.

One of my response filters, my *seen as helpful* filter, prevented me from expressing out loud my unspoken inside response. My *seen as helpful* filter reminded me that change is hard. Part of the value I bring to Derrick is helping him articulate what he has been afraid to admit even to himself, perhaps for a long time—such as his own feeling of responsibility for the mess the project was in. If Derrick had been able to articulate that for himself, he would have—and he would not have needed me.

So instead of blaming Derrick for not knowing what he pays me to know, I took a deep breath and said with patience, conviction, and compassion, "Derrick, I'm concerned for you and your project. I'm worried that if you proceed without understanding how you got into this mess, you could soon find yourself in another familiar and regrettable situation." That response was very different from my inside response.

My *seen as helpful* filter helped me respond to Derrick in a way that created more openness for him to listen to the implications of project history on any future project decisions. Derrick seemed to get it and provided me with the historical information I needed. Later, Derrick told me that my recommendations were more easily put into perspective knowing the project's history and were ultimately more useful to him.

Here are two more of my response filters, discussed in Chapter 3, with explanations of how they might impact my ability to give useful information:

1. *Don't celebrate too much or too soon* filter—When I really go for something and finally get it, this filter sometimes keeps me from expressing my joy, happiness, or excitement. I'm afraid that if I do express my positive emotion, the wonderful thing I got will go away, disappear, or be taken back.

   This filter could prevent me from publicly celebrating a project success, telling my management about my team's success, or sharing what worked and did not work with other project teams. If I do not give this information, I lose an opportunity to be a powerful advocate for my project. When I give this information, it can be useful for the following reasons:
   - Team members know they are acknowledged and appreciated for their efforts. They may become more positively motivated. When they know what they are doing well, they are more likely to keep doing it.
   - Management is more likely to understand the reasons for success. Management is responsible for many projects and is in a position to support and encourage the spread of suc-

cessful ideas and methods across project boundaries, but can do so only when aware of those ideas and methods.
- Other project teams can learn about tools, methods, and approaches that helped your project succeed. Sharing this kind of information contributes to the collective project wisdom of your organization.

2. *You must be stupid* filter—Whether I actually say it out loud or imply it with the questions I ask, I always feel bad after I use this response filter. It can slip out anywhere, anytime such as in:
   - Responding to a remark I perceive as unkind during a teleconference
   - Giving feedback on a draft document during a project planning meeting
   - Conducting a performance review of an employee who reports to me
   - Pointing out potential defects in a work product during a peer review.

   Okay, I admit that my evil twin may feel a nanosecond of righteousness. But that quickly disappears. The *you must be stupid* filter is not useful or helpful to anyone. Most often it results in stress, hurt, and anger, and tends to cut off any useful communication. Once it is used, the damage is done and cannot be undone. When I use it, this filter makes it extremely difficult for me to be a powerful advocate, advisor, and decision-maker for my project.

   I have tried pretending that I do not have this filter. I have also tried to sit on this filter—to repress it. Neither has worked. What has worked best for me is to accept this filter as part of me. At one time in my life, this filter was the best technique/method I had for protecting myself from feeling hurt and incompetent. Instead of trying to get rid of it, I have appreciated it for the protection it provided and have added another filter, my *generous interpretation* filter. With this filter, I look for the positive intention in what I see others doing. The more I use my *generous interpretation* filter, the less I seem to need my *you must be stupid* filter.

TECHNIQUE 4: START AND END WITH THANK YOU

"Thank you" acknowledges to the receiver that you noticed him and are thankful for something he has done, or perhaps will do. There is always an opportunity to say thank you for something. For example, if someone sends you an email with a question, you can start your reply with, "Thank you for your question." You might be thankful because the question gives you an opportunity to share your unique knowledge. You might be thankful simply because you like answering questions. Perhaps doing so makes you feel good, and that is something for which you can be thankful.

Many of us were taught to say "please" and "thank you" whether we want to or not because it is polite. We often do it automatically. I am not talking about that kind of thank you, which is automatic and clichéd. I am talking about a thoughtful and genuine thank you. A genuine thank you can:

- Enhance self-esteem for both you and the receiver
- Inform the receiver (if the thank you is specific and descriptive)
- Create a human connection with the receiver
- Make you and the receiver feel good (although the feeling might be a little awkward at first)
- Encourage collaborative relationships among project team members.

Also end your message with "thank you." You could be thankful in advance for something you requested from the receiver. Your thank you could simply be thanking the person for the opportunity to be in communication with him. When a person reads or hears your message, he at least can be thanked for the time he took to do that. Remember to end with "thank you."

TECHNIQUE 5: SEPARATE YOUR INTERPRETATION FROM YOUR OBSERVATION

It is human nature for us to interpret what we observe. Most of us do this almost automatically without thinking about it. We have to make a conscious effort not to. The problem comes when a receiver cannot distinguish the factual information from the interpretation. The interpretation then can unknowingly be taken as fact, and the receiver can be misinformed or misled. We may be completely unaware that we are mixing our interpretation with our observation because it is so automatic.

Here is an example of what I mean by mixing interpretation with observation:

"The go/no-go decision was made today. The decision is to delay go-live for two weeks. The delay reflects poorly on our team because we will miss our go-live milestone date."

The observations in this statement are: "The go/no-go decision was made today" and "The decision is to delay go-live for two weeks." Let's assume that both are accurate and factual. The interpretation part is: "The delay reflects poorly on our team because we will miss our go-live date." There can be other interpretations of the delay. One such interpretation is that our team is wise not to proceed with go-live if the risk it too high. If an interpretation is not labeled so, the receiver might be misled to believe that the interpretation is accurate and factual.

Interpretations provide information too. But they provide information about the giver, not necessarily about the observation. Try to omit your interpretations, or if that is too difficult, at least try to identify which is observation and which is interpretation. Notice the difference in this modified version of the earlier statement:

"The go/no-go decision was made today. The decision is to delay go-live for two weeks. To me, the delay reflects poorly on our team because we will miss our go-live milestone date. Other interpretations were expressed, however, including that our team is wise not to proceed with go-live because the risk is too high."

TECHNIQUE 6: GIVE THE CONTEXT WITH YOUR INFORMATION

If you have ever joined a conversation already in progress, missed the first 10 minutes of a movie, or started reading a novel in the middle, you know what it is like to get information without its context. The information's context helps the receiver make sense of the information. Information without its context can be confusing and difficult to evaluate. For example, consider this piece of information: "A man was shooting his machine gun." You may interpret this information differently if the context is that the man was a Drug Enforcement Administration officer in a shootout with a drug gang than if the man was a stranger having a psychotic break in a playground full of children.

Consider another piece of information: "This project failed." You might interpret this information differently if you knew that the purpose of the project was to make something fail. A piece of context that would make this information more useful would be a definition of failure and success. If this was a testing project, the definition of success might be to break some software. If the test plan and test scripts were not able to break the software, then the test project could be said to have failed. Is this good news or bad news, and to whom?

Information that is confusing and difficult to evaluate is not useful information.

At a minimum, try to package the information you give with the following:

- The purpose or reason you are giving the information to the receiver
- What you want the receiver to do with the information
- Any time constraints you know about
- Any conditions such as failure or success criteria
- Your role in giving the information
- How to contact you in case there are questions.

As the example about Jessica and the tax ID number in Chapter 12 indicated, the context for your information can be critical to gaining the cooperation and participation of the receiver.

TECHNIQUE 7: GIVE AN INFORMATION PICNIC

This technique provides a template for giving useful information. I use the picnic metaphor because it reminds me to include all the little extras besides the food itself, like napkins, forks, knives, condiments, tablecloth or blanket, trash bags, paper cups, paper plates, beverages, ice, music—all the things that make eating the food more enjoyable.

Some of the techniques presented thus far are like the picnic extras. They are in addition to the information being given and are intended to make the information more useful to the receiver.

Picnic item	Purpose	Example
Greeting	To make contact with the receiver—to acknowledge there is a real person to whom you want to give some useful information.	Cheryl, good to be in contact with you.
Thank you	To acknowledge to the receiver that you notice her and are thankful for something she has done, or perhaps will do.	Thank you for offering. I appreciate your willingness to review the draft Sizzling Serrano project plan.

Picnic item	Purpose	Example
Purpose and form of your message	To answer a question, deliver a proposal, ask a question, make a complaint, make a recommendation. Form includes: attachments to email, paper documents, and CDs. Also include instructions on what to do if the form is not readable by the receiver.	Per your request, I am enclosing the draft project plan. The plan is in both paper form and CD. If you have any problems viewing either, please let me know right away. I can resubmit either form, or use another form that works better for you.
Context of message	To indicate time, boundaries, your assumptions, your interpretation, situation, people, problems, issues, previous attempts and outcomes, or other parts of the context.	As you may know, this is the third attempt at the Serrano project. The previous two attempts failed.
Your message	To indicate what you want the receiver to do with your information.	Please scrutinize this draft. I will call you in a few days to set up a time when we can discuss your feedback and suggestions.
Intention, meaning, significance	To clarify what you mean and do not mean; to express the significance to you of this message; to express your intention in giving this message.	By scrutinize, I mean really examine it in detail, not just scan it. I will be much more confident in the plan with your input. I am hoping you will spot potential risks and opportunities based on your extensive experience with projects of this size and complexity.

Picnic item	Purpose	Exampl.e
Request for feedback, suggestions	To let the receiver know you that you want feedback and suggestions.	Cheryl, please give me your frank and honest feedback and suggestions.
Acknowledgment of receipt	To close the loop, in the event your message does not reach the receiver.	Please email me to let me know that you received this.
Close and thank you	To terminate this information picnic and thank the receiver.	I look forward to receiving your feedback. Thanks.
Signature and contact information	To let the receiver know who you are and how to contact you.	Jack Jack@serrano.hot 555.211.0008

TECHNIQUE 8: ALLOW FOR DRAFT REVIEW

This technique has saved my bacon more than once, especially when the information I am giving has potentially high significance to or impact on the receiver and the receiver's organization. Calling the information a draft enables the receiver to take an active role in shaping the information. It can also increase the receiver's acceptance and ownership of the information.

Using this technique can be a little tricky, though. Do not permit the draft to become an opportunity for endless iterations. One or two iterations will probably be enough, and set that expectation with the receiver at the beginning. Do not compromise your integrity by allowing the receiver to make changes with which you cannot agree.

One value of using the draft technique is that the receiver can become your guide to local culture. For example, she may tell you how to word the information so that it will be more understandable and acceptable to her and her organization. She may be able to advise you on the use of special terms and acronyms. She may let you in on implied protocols you don't know about—such as who else should see the information first and whom you should include in the distribution. Finally, she may let you know if something you have in your draft is inaccurate or misleading.

This technique can work well for many kinds of project-related documents, such as:

- Assessment reports
- Audits
- Contracts
- Management reports
- Project planning documents
- Project retrospective reports
- Project review reports
- Proposals
- Requirements documents
- Statements of work
- Status reports
- Test reports
- Work breakdown structures.

To recap:

- You can be a more powerful advocate, advisor, and decision-maker for your project when you give useful information.
- In this chapter, useful information means:
  - —Useful to the receiver (the person to whom you are giving the information).
  - —Information that has the potential to shape your project's context in a positive way.
- Eight practical techniques can help you increase your ability to give this kind of useful information:
  Technique 1: Consider whom you want to receive your information
  Technique 2: Consider the burden of perfection
  Technique 3: Use your awareness of your response filters
  Technique 4: Start and end with thank you
  Technique 5: Separate your interpretation from your observation
  Technique 6: Give the context with your information
  Technique 7: Give an information picnic
  Technique 8: Allow for draft review.

Try this:

1. Pick one of the eight techniques and use it the next time you give information to your colleague. Let your colleague know in advance

what you are doing. Ask your colleague for feedback on the technique you tried. What effect, if any, did it have on the usefulness of your information to your colleague?

2. Think about your past attempts to give project-related information. What comes to mind as some of your finest attempts? What, if any, effects do you know about that your information had on shaping your project's context?

Chapter 14

WHOM DOES YOUR PROJECT NEED TO PLEASE?

One critical element in shaping your project's context for success is meeting the expectations of people whom your project needs to please. Many project leaders focus their efforts on working within their project team to see that the project's technical work is completed. Of equal importance is knowing which people outside your project team must be pleased and how to deal with them and their expectations. This is something that many project leaders fail to pay enough attention to—perhaps because they underestimate its importance, perhaps because they feel less competent navigating this area, perhaps because this is hard information to get. But this element is critical: *Unmet, unclear, undiscovered expectations can sink your project.*

As a project leader, you need to find out:

- Whom you have to please
- What their expectations are
- What you must do to meet those expectations
- What you must do when any expectations are not met.

Here is a story from my colleague David Schmaltz that illustrates how undiscovered expectations can lead to dissatisfaction even when we are clear about the objective.[1]

Let's say that you and I agree to play singles tennis on Saturday at 9:00 AM. We meet at the appointed day and time. We play a full match. You win the match handily. For me it was great fun. For you it was awful. How can this be?

Our objective was to play a tennis match. Unbeknownst to me, you are a fierce competitor. I am not. You were expecting a killer competitive match. I

[1]E-mail, September 12, 2001.

was expecting to bang the ball around a bit and have fun. Your expectation of a killer competitive match was unmet. I had a great time, even though I lost. You had a horrible time, even though you beat me. To you, the match was a waste of time. To me, it was great fun. Had we discovered each other's expectations prior to playing, we might have had a very different game and outcome, or we might have decided not to play at all.

It can be like this with projects too. We may all agree on the project's objectives explicitly. We may even document them in writing. But our expectations of how we go about achieving the objectives may vary among individuals. Expectations are not typically discussed in advance and they are not usually captured in writing. As with the tennis match, it is possible to meet a project's objectives yet have a failed project because expectations were undiscovered and unmet.

Among the people your project needs to please are a special class of decision-makers. Mr. Schmaltz refers to them as people who in their role can say "no" to your project and make it stick. It is to your advantage to find out who these people are. Make contact with them and discover their expectations. Doing so is essential to shaping your project's context for success. Why? Because it is nearly impossible to satisfy unknown expectations. What about decision-makers who say "no" and get overruled or ignored? You may have to please them too, but give a higher priority to those who can say "no" to your project and make it stick.

With projects, it is possible to meet deliverables and deadlines yet not meet important but unknown expectations. The people having those unknown expectations might view your project as a failure even when it is successful by other standards. It is much easier to satisfy expectations that are known. Even so, you are not likely to satisfy them all. For this reason, handling unmet expectations is a very useful skill.

ACKNOWLEDGING YOUR EXPECTATIONS

Don't overlook that you are one of the people your project needs to please. What are your expectations, wants, and hopes for your project? When you allow yourself to acknowledge and own these fully, you keep yourself in the picture. It is much easier to lead your project when you are in the picture. Of course, this does not mean that all your expectations, wants, and hopes will be satisfied. There are always tradeoffs.

With which of your expectations, wants, and hopes do you stand firm? With which can you be flexible? When can you say "no" to your project and make it stick? If the answer is "never," your project may be leading you instead of you leading it. For example, you may expect that proposed changes to the scope of your project are subjected to a rigorous approval process that identifies impacts to schedule and resources. You might stand firm on saying "no" to scope changes in the absence of such an approval process. If you cannot say "no" and make it stick, and there is no scope change approval process, then your project is in danger of pleasing no one.

IDENTIFYING THE PEOPLE WHO CAN SAY "NO" AND MAKE IT STICK

Who are the people who can say "no" to your project and make it stick? What do they expect from your project? If you do not know who these people are, you are blind to a key part of your project's context. If you do not know what these people expect from your project, your project's success is significantly at risk.

Identifying these people is not difficult. You can sometimes find their signatures on key project documents such as project chartering documents, scope change requests, requirements documents, process flow documents, design documents, project funding documents, project budgets, user acceptance test plans, and go/no-go criteria checklists. People who approve these types of documents are people with whom you need to develop and maintain open and honest communications. You will need their cooperation and support. Your project needs to please these people.

In some organizations, key project documents do not exist. Even if such documents do exist, they do not always have signatures. The following examples of key project documents may be known by different names and may have different meanings depending on which project management or development methodologies are in use. I include brief descriptions of these documents so that:

1. If these documents do not exist in your organization, you at least know what function they serve and you can look for the individuals who serve a similar function in your organization.
2. If these documents do exist in your organization but have different names, you can recognize them by the functions they serve.

The individuals who sign these documents are of key importance.

Important project documents include:

- *Project charter*—a high-level management document that clarifies a business problem or opportunity and seeks approval to begin the next phase. The project charter precedes project definition and often enables project definition. Not every project charter will result in a project. Management may decide that a project is not feasible or that the business problem or opportunity can be addressed in some other way. People who sign project charters might include a senior business executive, a senior financial officer, and the chief information officer.

- *Scope change request*—a document used to control changes to the scope of the project. It typically contains a description of the proposed change, an explanation of why this change is necessary, estimated schedule and resource impact, and any dependencies upon other projects. People who sign scope change requests might include a project manager, project sponsor, project office director, quality assurance (QA) manager, and client or user representative.
- *Requirements document*—describes how the finished product must function, including: business functions performed, user interfaces, inputs, outputs, performance characteristics, and operating environments. Requirements documents typically contain approval signatures of a project manager, systems architect, QA manager, client or user representatives, and business client or user management.
- *Process flow diagram*—describes inputs, process steps, and outputs of a specific business process (e.g., hiring a new person) or a project process (e.g., changing the project scope). A process flow diagram typically contains approval signatures of business client or user management, project sponsors, business analysts, and a QA manager.
- *Design document*—a visual representation of the product to be built based on a translation of documented requirements. In the case of software, a design document is like a blueprint for coding. People who sign design documents might include a system architect, program office director, client or user representatives, QA manager, and/or project sponsors.
- *Project funding document*—details the governance, sources, amounts, and schedule of funding for a project. People who sign these documents might include a program office director, project sponsor, or financial officer.
- *Project budget*—documents the time-bound allocation of approved funds to specific project resources by line item. Typically, a budget line item corresponds to a WBS line item and usually covers a fiscal or calendar year time period. People who sign project budgets might include a project manager, external

implementation partner representative, program office director, project sponsor, and financial officer.

- *User acceptance test plan*—documents the tests to be completed and the acceptable results for each test, which will constitute goodness and acceptability of the product by the user or buyer. The user acceptance test is typically performed by users or user representatives. People who sign user acceptance test plans might include a program office director, project sponsor, QA manager, client or user representatives, and business client or user management.
- *Go/no-go checklist*—a tool used to make an informed decision to continue or stop the implementation of a major project milestone, such as "go-live" or "first ship." Criteria, measures, progress, and indicators on the checklist are typically agreed upon in advance by the decision-makers, who preside over a go/no-go meeting. People who rely on such a checklist might include a program office director, project manager, project sponsors, QA manager, and client or user management. (These people may or may not actually sign the checklist.)

TRACKING EXPECTATIONS

As you identify people your project needs to please, make time to meet with each one on a regular basis. If possible, try to establish a rhythm with these meetings—that is, same day, same time, same duration, same location on a repeating pattern (for example, the first and third Monday of each month from 3:00 to 3:30 PM in the same location of his or her choice). Your objective in the initial meeting with each person will be to discover as many expectations as you can.

These individuals sign many documents—indicating their approval of a proposal, their agreement to act on a recommendation, or their choice from among several alternatives. Their signature indicates their agreement. From a signature alone, you cannot know the individual's expectations.

Expectations are usually unexplored territory residing somewhere inside the individual's thoughts and feelings. Sometimes expectations are obvious to the person owning them—so obvious that it hardly seems necessary to express them. Sometimes expectations are out of the awareness of their owner. Both kinds of expectations can be discovered directly by asking open-ended questions. The general principle is to *make what is implicit explicit*.

As you meet with these people, you may discover conflicting expectations. This is a good thing! It is far better to discover and resolve conflicting expectations sooner rather than later. Sometimes just getting the parties together to discuss the conflicting expectations is all that is needed. Sometimes the conflicts may have to be resolved following the governance structure that has been set up for the project. For example, if the project has an oversight committee, that group might be able to arbitrate a resolution. Otherwise, the project executive sponsor may have to resolve the conflict.

Here are several examples of questions you may want to consider asking when you first meet with each individual. For these examples, let's say that you have determined that Paul is a person your project needs to please. These questions are appropriate for you, the project leader, to ask Paul either when starting up a new project or joining a project in progress. Write down the answers for future reference. Do not assume that Paul's answers will be the same as those of other individuals your project needs to please.

1. *How much of your own time do you expect will be required by this project?*
   This question allows you to gauge how important Paul perceives your project to be. Time is precious to Paul. The more important he perceives the project to be, the more time he will be willing to spend with it. Knowing the answer will help you put into perspective answers to the questions that follow.
2. *How do you expect to kept informed of progress?*
   This question allows you to discover Paul's preferences for form (written, verbal, email, other) and content (brief overview, details, exceptions only), as well as Paul's hot buttons. The answer will enable you to tailor progress reports to deliver exactly the right amount, type, and form of information that will be useful to him.
3. *What severity of problems requires your personal attention and how do you want to be notified?*
   This question allows you to set a threshold for problem severity below which you do not need to involve Paul. You might also want to ask Paul what his preference is for learning about problems below the threshold. The second part of this question will help you discover Paul's preferences for how he wants to be notified when the problem severity is above the threshold. For example, he may want to be paged immediately, or he may rather be notified by an email flagged as high priority.
4. *What type of information is helpful to you when a situation requires your personal attention?*
   This question allows you to find out what type of information Paul wants to know when a problem is severe enough to warrant his attention. Knowing this in advance may save your time

and his time because you will be prepared with the right information. You will not waste time trying to figure out which information Paul wants.

5. *Who should handle your project responsibility when you are not available?*
   Paul is likely a busy executive. He will not be available every time you need him. Ask Paul for a backup to handle his responsibilities during those times. It may be necessary for Paul to differentiate which kinds of responsibilities his backup can handle from those only Paul can handle. It is a good idea to agree in advance exactly what should happen if Paul is not available and no one else can cover his responsibility.
6. *Here is what is supposed to happen next on the X project; do you agree?*
   This question allows you to check your understanding with Paul regarding what happens next on the X project. If there is explicit agreement, a bump (i.e., an annoyance, irritation, or upset) may be avoided. Bumps can be minor or serious.
7. *Here is what is NOT supposed to happen next on the X project; do you agree?*
   This question allows you to further check your understanding with Paul by clarifying what is not supposed to happen as well. Obviously, it is better to get Paul's agreement in advance before it becomes an unmet expectation.
8. *What would you expect to see and hear if this project phase is successful?*
   Paul may have different ideas than you do about what success means for this project phase. Knowing his meaning of success will give you an opportunity to compare it with your own meaning and that of others your project needs to please. Identify and discuss any potential conflicts among these meanings.
9. *Which project documents do you expect to see?*
   Paul may not want to see every project status report, issue log, hill climbing chart, Gantt chart, or other project document produced on a regular basis. Paul's answer to this question will enable you to provide him with only the documents he really wants to see. Let Paul know that under special conditions you may provide additional documents. For example, if a critical milestone is in danger, you might want to provide additional documents that will help Paul grasp the seriousness of the issues.
10. *How are you expecting to see those project documents and how often?*
    Paul might want to see paper documents, electronic documents, or both. For instance, if you send him paper, but he

prefers email, he may miss time-critical information because he doesn't read his paper mail as often as his email. He may not want to view a weekly status report, preferring instead to see a monthly summary of project status. His preferred frequency may change during the project lifecycle, so it is good to check with him periodically to see if he has changed his preferences.

11. *What do you expect me to do when I believe your expectations are not going to be met?*
    This question gives you an opportunity to work out with Paul how you will deliver disappointing news. Ask him how he prefers to receive that kind of information. You may let Paul know your own concerns about being the bearer of such news. For example, he may prefer to receive the news initially via private email followed by a private conversation via telephone or in person.
12. *What other expectations might you have that we have not talked about yet?*
    The preceding questions and their subsequent discussions may trigger Paul to think of other expectations he didn't realize he had. This question will provide an opportunity for him to express those expectations.
13. *May I check with you periodically to see if your expectations are being met?*
    This question lets Paul know that you care about his expectations. Hopefully the answer will be yes. That way you can find out sooner than later if Paul has a problem with your project.
14. *May I check with you periodically to see if your expectations have changed?*
    This question also lets Paul know that you care about his expectations. It acknowledges and honors Paul's ability to change his expectations over time. If the answer is yes, this will help you stay on the same page with Paul.

HANDLING UNMET EXPECTATIONS

When you are on the receiving end of someone else's unmet expectations, you may be surprised by the range and intensity of emotions that come into play—both yours and the other person's. Unmet expectations very often lead to bumps. In the heat of the moment, it may be difficult for you to stay in your own "hula hoop."

I first heard the hula hoop metaphor from my colleague Jean McLendon.[2] The image is that each of us has our own hula hoop

[2]E-mail, August 25, 2000.

(picture the wildly popular toy of the 1950s). When I'm standing inside my hula hoop, this represents my being in awareness of my boundaries and my full sense of my whole self—separate and distinct from any other person. As long as I stay in my own hula hoop, I can move about freely among others and their hula hoops. But when I try to step into someone else's hula hoop, we become entangled. I can become confused about which is my responsibility and which is the other person's responsibility.

As an example of stepping into the other person's hula hoop, I might start feeling that my expectations should be the same as the other person's and I should be upset also. Another example might be that I start feeling that I am responsible for the other person's upset and immediately try to make him or her stop feeling that way. Doing either could easily escalate the upset without getting to the heart of the matter.

Here are some tips for handling unmet expectations while staying in your own hula hoop.

Let's assume that it is Monday afternoon and Paul has just told you he is disappointed and angry because he expected the scheduled go-live this morning and it did not happen. You are aware that Paul expected go-live this morning. What do you do?

- Breathe. Breathing is very important because it provides oxygen to your brain. When you stop breathing or your breathing is shallow and fast, as sometimes happens when you are dealing with emotionally charged situations, your oxygen-deprived brain does not function as well; thus, you may not be thinking clearly and you may go blank. Take a couple of deep breaths.
- Remember that it is okay for Paul to expect go-live this morning. That does not mean that he will get go-live this morning. It does not mean that you should expect go-live this morning. It does not mean that you should feel guilty because go-live did not happen. Paul is entitled to feel what he feels—disappointment and anger. You are entitled to have your own feelings, which may or may not include disappointment and anger. It does not mean that you should try to get Paul to stop feeling disappointed and angry.
- Breathe.
- Acknowledge Paul's feelings. Try saying something like, "I understand that you feel disappointed and angry by this situation. What do you want to do with your disappointment and anger?" Wait for Paul's response.
- Breathe.
- Acknowledge your own feelings and express them. For example, you might feel relieved because you know that the system was not

ready for go-live today. If so, say that. Paul might agree had he attended the go/no-go meeting last Friday. All the key stakeholders agreed after reviewing the go/no-go checklist that several problems needed to be resolved. Go-live was postponed one week.

- Breathe.
- Be factual and truthful. Tell Paul what you know of the go/no-go checklist discussions. If you are not sure about a fact, say so. If you think the decision to postpone was correct, say so.
- Breathe.
- Do not hide anything. Be willing to answer all of Paul's questions to the best of your ability. At the same time, you do not have to tell him everything you know, especially that which is not relevant, that which is hearsay, or that which you have promised to keep confidential or private.
- Breathe.
- Do not sugarcoat the situation. If you try to make the situation seem less serious, Paul could construe that you think he should not feel disappointed and angry or that you think he is overreacting. Let Paul own his reactions. If you think the situation is less serious, own that and say it. But do not try to convince Paul that he should think the same as you do or that he should not feel what he feels.
- Breathe.
- Problem-solve. Do not blame or placate. Do not accept Paul either blaming or placating you. Identify the problem to be solved, brainstorm potential solutions, involve Paul in evaluating solutions, choose the best solution, and let Paul know what next steps will be taken. In the case of go-live, tell Paul how the decision to postpone was made and what actions are being taken so that the system will be ready for go-live next week.

STACKING THE DECK IN YOUR PROJECT'S FAVOR

Your project needs a lot of help to please the people it needs to please. You alone cannot always prevent things from going wrong. That is why it is important to build solid relationships with the people your project needs to please. Solid relationships can withstand things going wrong. You cannot build solid relationships by hiding out in your work space and pinging emails. Relationship work requires some face time with each person.

You can stack the deck in your project's favor if you:

- Discover whom your project needs to please.
- Discover the expectations of those individuals.

- Check those expectations periodically to see if they are being met or have changed.
- Handle unmet expectations as soon as possible in a caring and respectful way.

To recap:

- Find out whom your project needs to please. One such group is those people who can say "no" to your project and make it stick.
- You can sometimes find such people by their signatures on key project documents.
- Once you identify these people, meet with them and find out their expectations of your project. Stay connected with them because their expectations can change.
- Remember that you are one of the people your project needs to please. Honor your own expectations for your project.
- The ability to handle unmet expectations is important because it is unrealistic to think that all expectations, even the ones you know about, will be met.
- You can stack the deck in your project's favor by building solid relationships with the people your project needs to please. Solid relationships can withstand things going wrong, as they inevitably will.

Try this:

1. Make a list of the people who can say "no" to your project and make it stick. As you look at your list, try to imagine each person's expectations of your project. Write these down. Compare your imagined expectations with what you eventually discover are each person's expectations after meeting with him or her. How close are they?
2. Try to identify those expectations that you perceive to be high risk (i.e., less than 50 percent chance that they will be met). Make a plan for how you will handle these expectations if they are not met.
3. Write down your own expectations for your project. How many are being met? Notice your emotional response as you consider each expectation and whether it is being met. What changes, if any, would you like to make for yourself? For your project?

Chapter 15

SUBSTITUTES FOR TIME

Time pressure is a tyrant and he is oppressive. He seems to be a constant companion of your project's context. However, a powerful project leader has special powers to tame the time pressure tyrant. Certain ideas and techniques can help you acquire the special powers you'll need to tame the tyrant:

- See the tyrant for who he really is.
- Reframe time.
- Use substitutes for time.

WHERE DOES TIME PRESSURE COME FROM?

For me, time pressure is an internal response to my interpretation of an external stimulus, such as a deadline that I have accepted. Yes, the pressure comes from *inside me*. If I allow it, time pressure sets a trap for me. Here is the bait that can lure me into my own trap:

- I want to do a good job.
- I perceive that "good" means finishing by the due date.
- I perceive that "bad" means not finishing by the due date.
- I perceive that I do not have enough time to meet the deadline.
- I believe that I can't renegotiate the deadline.

Can you see how I might feel trapped? When I trap myself in this way, I often fear that I will be seen as too slow, incompetent, a slacker, or not a team player if I don't meet the deadline. Is this a familiar trap for you? Perhaps you share some of my fears or maybe you have your own uncomfortable feelings about time pressure. For me, the pressure seems to be coming from the outside, when in fact I'm pressuring myself. I am my own time pressure tyrant!

One way to free myself from my time pressure trap is to reexamine my perceptions and beliefs around time and doing a good job, perhaps with the help of a supportive friend who simply reminds me of what I know from my experience. I keep my self-esteem kit close by.[1] My kit contains my wisdom box, courage stick, golden key, wishing wand, detective's hat, and the heart (see Chapter 2 for more about the self-esteem kit). The icons remind me to access my internal resources, which are always there: wisdom, courage, opening doors, wishes, exploration, and feelings.

Reexamining my perceptions and beliefs might go like this:

I perceive that "good" means finishing by the due date.

But there are other aspects of "good," such as quality of work product, cost, or relationship with the client or user. Sometimes finishing by the due date can ultimately be bad—if quality, cost, or relationship suffer too much as a result. I use the wisdom box and the golden key for this one.

I perceive that "bad" means not finishing by the due date.

Sometimes it can be "bad" to finish by the due date. If you have ever felt the pain of implementing a system before it is ready, you know what I mean. Asking for more time to be sure the system is ready is a sign of project management maturity. Think through the consequences of a premature finish: What is likely to happen? What are the costs? I use the wisdom box and the golden key for this one.

I perceive that I do not have enough time to meet the deadline.

If the deadline seems arbitrary or not backed up by credible estimates, I may probe a bit more into the scope and estimating methods and assumptions. After the probing, I'll probably be either more comfortable or more uncomfortable with the deadline. Regardless of which, I'm always glad when I investigate further. For example, I may learn which tradeoffs could be made between schedule and functionality. Knowing this can help me make better decisions for the

---

[1]Virginia Satir, et al., *The Satir Model, Family Therapy and Beyond* (Palo Alto: Science and Behavior Books, Inc., 1991), pp. 293-297.

project and offer better advice to the project team. I use the courage stick and the detective's hat for this one.

I believe that I can't renegotiate the deadline.

Everything is always negotiable if I know my bottom line—for example, I am ready to walk away to protect my integrity. The more informed I make myself about the scope and estimating assumptions, the more I can question the reasonableness of estimates, scope, and cost with respect to the deadline. I know that if I accept an unreasonable deadline, I help no one and I put myself in a no-win situation. I use the courage stick and the heart for this one.

Although it is useful to examine each of these individually, I find that there is a positive synergystic effect when I examine all my project fears, traps, perceptions, and beliefs together. The synergy comes from the interrelationships of all these elements. The synergy also comes from the interaction of my internal resources (e.g., courage and wisdom integrated are more powerful than courage alone and wisdom alone).

REFRAMING TIME

Another way to tame the tyrant is to change how you view time. Try a different frame. Changing the frame can change how you see time, much like changing the frame on a picture changes how you see the picture. Some of us perceive time as concrete, inflexible, and finite. After all, time is the passing of seconds, minutes, hours, days, weeks, months, and years. Once a minute passes, I can't get it back. I am one of those people who perceive time as abstract, flexible, and infinite. For example, can I see time? Does 10 seconds of free fall from an airplane seem the same as 10 seconds of commercial time on your television? Is there an end to time? Time sure feels finite when my project is late and getting later.

I would like to offer a different way of framing time. Call it substitutes for time. We may not know how to get time back once it passes, but consider the effects when we change how we choose to spend time. This frame involves substituting one kind of behavior for another, which will have a net effect on time. It is possible to get more time from our time by using substitutes for time, paradoxical as that may seem.

Consider this substitute for time: *slowing down*. You may have experienced that rushing sometimes results in more defects, which in turn take more time to fix. Slowing down may seem counterintuitive when you are under pressure, but try reframing this as avoiding wasted time from fixing defects caused by going too fast.

As an example, Team A and Team B are each given the same 4 hours to make a simple product. The product must be defect-free. All aspects of both teams are very similar such that neither team has an advantage or disadvantage. Team A works at a very fast pace to make its product, and finishes in 3.5 hours. Team A then begins to fix the three defects in its finished product. Each defect takes 1/2 hour to fix. Total time for Team A to make a defect-free product is 5 hours.

Team B starts out at the same pace as Team A, then consciously slows down the pace. At the end of 4 hours, Team B has just finished making its product. Team B's product has one defect. That defect takes 1/2 hour to fix. Total time for Team B to make a defect-free product is 4.5 hours.

The net effect on time of slowing down is that Team B has 1/2 hour to use at its discretion.

SUBSTITUTES FOR TIME

My partner, Eileen, and I once made *Substitutes for Time* decks of cards to give away as gifts to clients. It was a labor of love. Our hope was that the decks would help our clients deal more effectively with their time pressure, and thus avoid some of the pain and suffering. Eileen formatted and printed sheets of cards on heavy stock. I cut them out with scissors. Each deck had 26 cards, each with a different substitute for time printed on it. We included six blank "wild" cards so that the owner of the deck could add his or her own substitutes for time. Here are the cards currently in each deck:

"Wild"	"Wild"	"Wild"	"Wild"
Clear decision-making	Documentation	Delegating	Slowing down
Clear thinking	Repeatable process	Teamwork	Clear communication
Courage	Focus	Health	Priorities
Right number of staff	Reuse	Observing	Clear roles and responsibilities
Sleeping	A well-timed jiggle	"Wild"	"Wild"
Trust	The right tools	Your real "no"	Planning
Your real "yes"	Support	Exercise	Asking for help

One way to use the deck is to shuffle and deal three cards face down to each person on your team (including yourself). The number of cards dealt can be varied depending on the number of people on your team. The person to the left of the dealer turns over one card and reads it out loud, e.g. "planning." That person comments on how planning could be a substitute for time in the current project situation. The others in turn can comment or pass on how planning could be a substitute for time. Then the next person turns over a card, followed by a round of comments. This process is repeated until all the cards have been turned over and commented on. A wild card provides an opportunity for someone on the team to add a new substitute for time to the deck. The hope is that the cards and comments can trigger some useful ideas about how to get more time out of time.

Trust can be a substitute for time. I've noticed in my work with teams that some new teams spend a large amount of time on what I call team overhead—time spent by team members learning to trust each other. Examples are time spent checking status, time spent checking quality, and time spent on tasks that could be handled by someone else. Team overhead seems a natural, though time-consuming, human process and does provide useful checks and balances. As team members learn to trust each other, the amount of time spent on status and quality checks is reduced appropriately. Team members begin to trust each other enough to share some task responsibilities. The time no longer being spent on team overhead can be redirected toward other work.

Focus can be a substitute for time. When my time is split among several tasks (e.g., 20% on project x task, 50% on project y task, 30% on project z task), some time and focus will be lost as I switch between those tasks. A rule of thumb Jerry Weinberg uses when estimating the effects of splitting tasks is shown in the following table:

Task Splitting

Number of Tasks	Percent of time spent on each
1	100
2	40
3	20
4	10
5	5
more than 5	random

Material reprinted by permission of Dorset House Publishing from *Quality Software Management, Vol. 1: Systems Thinking,* p. 284.

This table says that with five tasks you could spend 75 percent of your time switching among tasks and 25 percent total completing the tasks. This has implications for project staffing. When a person is spread over several tasks, even though he may be 100 percent allocated, that does not mean he will be 100 percent productive. Consider extending the estimated duration of each task to compensate for switching. When possible, focus on fewer tasks to reduce the startup and shutdown time spent switching among tasks.

A well-timed jiggle can be a substitute for time. A jiggle is an action designed to shake things up a bit so as to get them unstuck. Individuals and teams can become stuck, doing the same behaviors over and over yet expecting different results. Jiggles often seem irrelevant at the time, and are hardly ever appreciated in the moment. Later, if the jiggle is successful, people are often grateful to the jiggler for helping them get unstuck.

Here is a jiggle example.

I conducted a project review for a client, Jeff, whose multimillion dollar project was out of control. Jeff, the senior executive sponsor, was in chaos as we sat in his office. His face was white and his palms were sweaty. We had just come from a project management meeting. The project director and his project managers were very upset by my review report and they seemed ready to riot. He said, "I guess I have made a lot of trouble for this project by bringing you in to tell us the truth." Jiggling, I said, "Jeff, that is one way to look at it." Jeff replied, his voice cracking, "There is another?" I said, "Yes, perhaps the trouble has been here for a long time, and now you are straightening it out." Jeff took a couple of deep breaths. His skin pinked. His voice became strong again. After a minute or so, he said very confidently, "You are absolutely right. We have all been in denial for long enough. The truth was difficult to hear, but now we know what we need to do to get this the project back under control. Excellent!"

This was a rather large jiggle for Jeff. Jiggles can be small too, such as turning on the air conditioning to cool off a meeting room that is too warm because no one can figure out how to lower the furnace thermostat.

Asking for help can be a substitute for time. Ask someone who has the knowledge or skill to answer your question or help you solve your problem. I have a part of me that wants to "do it myself." That part used to be so strong that I would automatically spend a lot of time muddling through by trial and error. I thought I had no choice. I appreciated the learning I acquired afterward, but the time it took was often more costly than I could afford. I still have that part, but now I choose when to use it and when not to use it. Sometimes, when I choose to, I can save time by asking for help.

Clear communication can be a substitute for time. Misunderstanding and confusion lead to mistakes. Mistakes take time to correct. Much of the time, we iterate communication until we get it right. By iterate, I mean we clarify what we mean over several interactions after we realize that the other person did not get the meaning we intended. The time to iterate plus the time to fix resulting mistakes can be costly. It may take a little more time on the front end to understand and to be understood clearly. But taking that time may mean fewer iterations plus fewer mistakes, which can add up to a net time saving.

The problem is that many of us think we are good communicators. If there is a miscommunication, it must be the other guy. Regardless of who miscommunicated, there is a cost. I think the cost can be lowered by spending a little more time checking understanding on the first iteration.

Clear decision-making can be a substitute for time. Have you ever experienced what seemed like hours of hashing over the same ideas in a project meeting with no decision in sight? Perhaps you have experienced what you thought was a decision, only to find out later that it was not. With some projects it is difficult to get any decision made. Even if a decision is made, it can later be ignored, overturned, or redecided ad nauseum.

I am not proposing that decisions should never be reviewed or changed. There is a difference between responsibly reviewing decisions and what I often see as a pattern of decision avoidance and/or chronic revisiting of decisions. How much time would you guess could be saved if projects had clear decision-making and the resulting decisions stuck?

Here are a few things you can do to have an impact if you are in this situation:

- In meetings, try to clarify the purpose of the meeting. If the purpose is to make a decision, there should be a clearly written statement of the decision to be made, the appropriate people to make the decision should be present, and attendees should have the information they need to make the decision.
- Once made, document decisions in writing so that they can be reviewed for understanding and later used as a reference.
- If you plan to take specific actions based on a decision, document your proposed actions in writing and check for understanding with those who might be affected.

- Train decision-makers using a commercially available decision-making training program.

Clear roles and responsibilities can be a substitute for time. Without clear roles and responsibilities, gaps and redundancy can develop. Both of these can lead to unpleasant surprises.

Gaps can result in important tasks not being completed by anyone. When a gap is discovered, each unassigned task and the time to complete it will have to be added to someone's workload.

Redundancy means more than one person unknowingly working on the same task. Some projects, for example, may intentionally use a redundant approach to produce a design. Redundancy, even when intentional, represents an efficiency loss. If person A and person B are both working on the same task unknowingly, some efficiency will be lost because person A or B could be using that time to complete other important tasks. Projects that intentionally use the redundant approach are willing to accept some inefficiency in hopes of developing a more robust design.

Clear thinking can be a substitute for time. Lots of things can affect our ability to think clearly. Illness, emotional upsets, too little or too much stress, alcohol, and some prescription drugs are a few that can have temporary negative physiological impacts on our brains. Breathing can help greatly. Breathing increases oxygen to the brain. When you use alcohol or prescription drugs, use them at times you do not need to think clearly (if there are such times). Take a little time to rest, breathe, and center yourself. The time you invest to achieve clear thinking can save you time in the long run.

Courage can be a substitute for time. One fascinating observation I often make from conducting project retrospectives is that project team members seem to know a project is in trouble long before the trouble becomes undeniable. Their ways of knowing vary. Some feel it in their gut. Some dream it. Some have a hunch or intuition. Others get headaches. Yet nobody expresses these feelings, dreams, hunches and headaches. Why?

For many, there is no safe forum for such information to be shared. Sometimes this information cannot be proven with facts. When projects start to go out of control, they often unconsciously develop a culture of *don't ask and don't tell.* Especially don't give bad news. This is exactly the opposite of what is needed to bring the project back into control. The seeds of recovery are to be found in the unexpressed feelings, dreams, hunches, and headaches of project team members.

It takes courage to buck the culture and express your individual concerns. Nobody likes to be the first to express such concerns, but doing so gives others permission to do the same. Why wait until the project retrospective to hear others say, "Yep, I had the same concerns, but I thought I was the only one." A little courage at the right time can prevent weeks, months, perhaps even years of denial.

Delegating can be a substitute for time. Free up your time by arranging to give some of your work to others. Usually, the others are subordinates, but they could also be teammates, even peers. Delegating is not the same as dumping. With delegating, you design a problem for someone else to solve. When you do not design it, like when you just dump it, you challenge fate.

Here are some things to consider when designing a problem for someone else to solve:

- Genuinely want him or her to succeed.
- Consider how would you design this problem for yourself.
- Do not ask him to do something he is not capable or willing to do.
- Verify with him at the beginning that your desired outcomes are understood.
- Be precise about *what*; leave *how* to his creativity.
- Answer questions; do not hover or take over.

Documentation can be a substitute for time. Some of us write important information down so that we do not have to remember it or recreate it every time we need it. Some of us like recreating information. When I am not pressed for time, I prefer to play with a new application or device to understand it rather than read a user manual. When I'm in a hurry, I go for the documentation.

Years ago as a coder, I enjoyed the challenge of debugging code without embedded comments. It was too easy if the code was well-documented with comments. Unfortunately, my boss did not appreciate trading time for my enjoyment. Whether it is code, an application, or a device, good documentation can save time—especially if multiple people have to use the code, application, or device repeatedly.

Exercise can be a substitute for time. Regular exercise can improve cardiovascular performance and muscle tone. Besides contributing to overall better health, exercise helps me manage my stress and returns me to a more centered state. When I am centered, I can think more creatively and am less likely to make errors of heart and mind. Fewer errors translates into less time spent correcting them.

Health can be a substitute for time. This is a simple one, but not easy. When I am healthy, I typically have more energy. I can use my extra energy to accomplish more work in the same amount of time. I miss fewer days of work due to illness so I can get more work done overall in the same calendar time period.

Observing can be a substitute for time. Improving my observation skills can save me time. There is always way more information surrounding me than what I actually notice. Have you ever wandered around in a mall or department store looking for the restrooms? When I finally ask an employee, he points and says, "That way, sir." Only then do I notice the huge sign on the wall, RESTROOMS.

When I am discussing a serious topic with a person, if I am skilled enough, I might notice signs such as facial expressions, tone of voice, inflection, breathing, and skin color. These are referred to as the person's "affect." Sometimes the words do not match the affect. If I check out the difference between the words and the affect, I might learn something that will save time later. For example, I may ask Jane, "Jane, do you want to join my project team?" Jane may say, "Sure." If I observe a mismatch between Jane's word, "sure," and her affect—perhaps tone of voice—then I will check that out. I want to be sure that Jane really wants to join my project. If you have ever had someone on your team who did not want to be there, you know how time-consuming and frustrating that can be.

Planning can be a substitute for time. Planning is one way to organize, sequence, and communicate tasks and contingencies directed toward achieving some future purpose or objectives. Planning can avoid time wasted due to:

- Performing the wrong tasks
- Not performing the right tasks
- Performing the right tasks, but in the wrong sequence
- Understaffing or overstaffing
- Not having supplies, materials, and tools when needed.

Plans and planning are two entirely different things. A plan is a map. Planning is the ability to make a map. The latter is more valuable because your project will change over time, requiring you to make a new map.

Priorities can be a substitute for time. When you have ten 1-hour tasks of equal importance and 10 hours to complete them, you may not need to prioritize. If you do not know how long each task will take, and some tasks are more important than others, you increase your chances of getting the most important tasks done before you run out of time by prioritizing. This is a bit like stealing. You steal time from less important tasks to ensure that the more important tasks are completed. The less important tasks get the remaining time, if any.

This is a self-correcting problem because as soon as the number one priority is completed, the number two priority becomes number one. The number three priority becomes number two and so on. On some projects I have observed a sort of mutant variation priority scheme. Everything is priority one! Operationally, when everything is priority one, there is no priority. This situation is never very productive, although some comfort can be taken in that everyone can shout, "Mine is first priority!" This is the time tyrant working everybody against each other.

A repeatable process can be a substitute for time. There are a number of benefits to using a repeatable process, including time. Take code inspections, for example. Following the same inspection process each time enables you to save time training the participants. Participants know what to expect and can concentrate more on the technical content and less on the process. If the process changes each time, participants have to concentrate both on learning a new process and the technical content being inspected.

Over time, you can redirect the time saved by not having to learn a new inspection process each time toward measuring and improving your inspection process. If you use a different process each time, you lose some ability to measure and improve it. If you plan to use defect data from your inspection process to analyze and improve your development methods, it is administratively easier to do when the data are in a consistent format. Formats may vary among different inspection processes, resulting in time-consuming apples and oranges comparisons.

Reuse can be a substitute for time. The claims of object-oriented methods and software component methods are well-known. I do not promote or defend the claims, preferring instead to say something safe in consultantese like, "It depends." I know for myself that reusing proposals, articles I've written, reports, templates, and other documents has saved me many hours of work. I charge a lot of money for an hour of my time, so this also saves my clients money.

The right number of staff can be a substitute for time. The right number of staff is somewhere between too few and too many. I do not know any magic incantations that can divine this number correctly. I think we all have a lot more to learn about the variables associated with calculating this number.

Too few staff needs a context to make any sense. Such a context might include a project scope and a deadline which, when compared to the given staff and their skill sets, adds up to too few. Too many staff also needs a context to make sense. One such context might include a project slipping schedule badly and a management decision to suddenly throw an army of developers at it. This context has already been written about by Frederick P. Brooks in *The Mythical Man-Month: Essays on Software Engineering*. Brooks' law tells us that adding people late in a project actually increases the amount of work to be done.

Sleeping can be a substitute for time. According to the National Institute of Neurological Disorders and Stroke website, "sleep appears necessary for our nervous systems to work properly. Too little sleep leaves us drowsy and unable to concentrate the next day. It also leads to impaired memory and physical performance and reduced ability to carry out math calculations. . . .Activity in parts of the brain that control emotions, decision-making processes, and social interactions is drastically reduced during deep sleep, suggesting that this type of sleep may help people maintain optimal emotional and social functioning while they are awake."[2] Deep sleep is also referred to as stage 4 sleep, during which the brain produces very slow delta waves. When the potential for errors and wasted time due to sleep deprivation exceeds the benefits of pulling an all-nighter, sleeping can be the counterintuitive yet correct approach.

Support can be a substitute for time. Ever drive yourself and others crazy for days or weeks over an important problem or dilemma? Do you vacillate? hesitate? cogitate? ventilate? If so, consider asking for support. Find someone you trust to act as a sounding board, give you feedback, mentor you, or just sit quietly with you while you think out loud.

Even your detractors can give you a different yet valuable kind of support. Detractors can be your sandpaper. Sandpaper can smooth rough edges. It can also rough up a smooth surface so it will take the next coat of finish, resulting in an even smoother surface.

Support can free you from your straightjacket. You can eventually free yourself, but support will help you do it quicker.

Teamwork can be a substitute for time. Ever notice how much time it takes for a team to gel? Teamwork involves two simultaneous activities. One is obvious and it is content-based: Teams develop prod-

---

[2]www.ninds.nih.gov/health_and_medical/pubs/understanding_sleep_brain_basic_.htm, September 15, 2000.

ucts—software, systems, services, hardware. At the same time, though, teams develop their ability to work together. This one is not so obvious and it is process-based. If you consider the process-based time an investment, then you will want to leverage that ability to work together on future projects. Having achieved the ability to work well together, teams amaze themselves with how little time it takes to solve problems compared to when they were in their early forming stage.

The right tools can be a substitute for time. Back in the early 1970s I wrote my own hierarchical DBMS for Xerox Corporation Sigma-9 computers using Fortran and Assembler language. I needed it for a serial number parts inventory system I was developing. I could have saved weeks, perhaps months, of time had I been able to purchase a commercially available DBMS.

Sometimes the right tool does not exist. Sometimes the right tool does exist, but it is not available to you, either because it is out of your awareness or it is just not accessible to you. Before I learned how to use a popular spreadsheet application, I used to use the Tables feature of a word processing application to create financial statements. I spent so much time summing and resumming columns and rows of numbers that I was powerfully motivated to learn a spreadsheet application.

Your real "no" can be a substitute for time. Ever say yes when you mean no? Sure, in our culture we sometimes do it to be polite or to avoid disappointing someone. Such a yes is usually not very convincing. Your words may be saying yes, but your body and your voice tone may not match your words. This can be confusing to others. It can lead you down a path you might regret. Every time you say yes when you mean no, you bruise your integrity a little. Saying your real no can protect your integrity and avoid time spent going down a regrettable path.

Suppose you are in a project meeting with your boss, your boss' boss, and your project sponsor. Your boss looks at you and says, "We need this project completed in six months. You are the project leader, will you commit to that?" You know in your deepest way of knowing that given the project's scope and the resources you have at your disposal, this project will take 12 months.

Inside you are saying no, but you feel pressure to say yes. Leading this project could be an opportunity to demonstrate your abilities. Saying no can be a career-limiting move. But if you say yes, the project will surely fail and that will be career-limiting too. You look at your boss and say, "Thank you for asking. No. As it currently stands, I cannot commit to that." Then you stop talking and wait for a response.

When you say your real no, it will be clear to others, not confusing. You feel no on the inside, you look and sound no on the outside, and your words match. Your real no is unmistakable. It comes from your wisdom box. You are now in a position to negotiate a more realistic project scope and deadline, one you can live with.

Your real "yes" can be a substitute for time. Ever say no when you mean yes? Sure, in our culture we sometimes do it to be polite or to avoid disappointing someone. Such a no is usually not very convincing. Your words may be saying no, but your body and your voice tone may not match your words. This can be confusing to others. It can lead you down a path you might regret.

Every time you say no when you mean yes, you bruise your integrity a little. Saying your real yes can protect your integrity and avoid time spent going down a regrettable path.

Suppose you are in a meeting with your boss, your boss' boss, and someone introduced to you as a project sponsor. Your boss looks at you and says, "We need this new project completed in six months. If we give this project to you, will you commit to that deadline?" This is an opportunity you have been waiting for. You have known about this potential project for several weeks. The project is highly visible and very important strategically to your company's success. You believe that the project can be completed in about six months.

Inside you are very excited. You are also torn. You will have to commute for six months, being home only for weekends. This will be difficult on you and your family. You have discussed this possibility with them and they are willing to make the sacrifices. You could say no with good reasons, but it probably would not sound convincing. Later you might regret it or even become resentful because you did not say yes. This project seems right for you. You take a deep breath. You look at your boss and say, "Thank you. Yes. I want the project and I will commit to this deadline." Then you stop talking and wait for a response.

When you say your real yes, it will be clear to others, not confusing. You feel yes on the inside, you look and sound yes on the outside, and your words match. Your real yes is unmistakable. It comes from your wisdom box.

To recap:

- My time pressure comes from inside me, although I like to think it comes from outside. I have met my time pressure tyrant and he is me!
- One way to free myself from my time pressure trap is to examine my perceptions and beliefs about time and what it means to do a good job. I do this with a supportive friend. This helps me tame my tyrant.
- Another way to tame my time pressure tyrant is to change how I perceive time by reframing it. I can change how I spend time and benefit from the resulting net effects on time.
- Get more time from your time by using *substitutes for time.*

Try this:

1. Use one or more substitutes for time. Write down the net effects on time that you observe for each one you try.
2. Try using the wild cards to add your own substitutes for time to the card deck.
3. Write in your journal or talk with a friend about what traps you into becoming your own time pressure tyrant.
4. Gather your project team over lunch and start a discussion about substitutes for time.

Chapter 16
INFRASTRUCTURE

Most of the time I do not think about infrastructure much at all. Infrastructure generally means the basic underlying framework or structure of a system. To a city or town, infrastructure means streets, sewers, electrical power, water, telephone lines, public transportation, schools, police, fire protection, hospitals, sanitation, city management, and a taxation structure to fund all of the above. If all these things are working reasonably well, I do not have to think about them. That's the thing about infrastructure—it is part of our context. If it is working, it is usually out of our awareness.

To enterprise information systems, infrastructure might mean networks, telecom, production hardware and software platforms, development hardware and software platforms, disaster recovery facilities, emergency backup power, servers, software licenses, software distribution, and technical support. Again, as long as these things work reasonably well, those who depend on them do not think about them much.

So, with cities and enterprises, infrastructure roughly means those things that we depend on that we do not think about much. Infrastructure seems to have the following characteristics:

- We need it to achieve our goals.
- It is part of our context, although perhaps not in the foreground of our awareness.
- We tend to take it for granted.

I think it is useful to apply this meaning of infrastructure and its characteristics more broadly—for example, to anything we might need to achieve our individual and project goals. I say more about the value of doing so a little later. First, here is a story to illustrate what I mean.

I was a day late sending my son a birthday card. I spoke with him by telephone, and promised him I would mail his birthday card immediately. My plan was to drive up to the local card shop, buy a suitable card, and drop it in the mailbox outside the card shop. I was in a hurry. I climbed into my car and started the engine. Then I realized I had no stamp for the card. I turned off the engine and climbed out of my car. I went back into my house and found a stamp to take with me. I got back into my car. Then I realized that I did not have a check to put with the card. I went back in the house and wrote a check to take with me. I got back in the car and started the engine. Guess what? I did not have my son's dorm address memorized, so I went back a third time, printed his address from my contact database, and got back into my car. This time, having everything I needed to complete my project successfully, I finally drove to the card shop and achieved my goal.

I was frustrated with all the back and forth. However, I would have been even more frustrated had I driven to the card shop without stamp, check, and address. The stamp, check, and address were the part of the infrastructure I needed to achieve my goal because:

- I could not mail the card without them.
- They were not in the foreground of my awareness in the context of preparing a birthday card in my car as opposed to in my home.
- I usually prepare birthday cards at my desk, which has stamps, checks, and addresses, so I took all that for granted momentarily.

In this simple example, I see the same kind of frustration as I see frequently on both large and small projects: the frustration of suddenly realizing, perhaps too late, that you do not have what you need to achieve your project's goals. The value of applying this broader meaning of infrastructure is:

- We can give a name to all the stuff we need, but may not think about.
- Naming that stuff means that we can plan for it.
- Infrastructure can apply to an individual, a project team, a single task, or a multitask project.

GREASING THE SKIDS

The old phrase "greasing the skids" has some relevance to my broader meaning of infrastructure. Grease reduces friction. Skids slide better with a little grease. Providing the right infrastructure for your project is like greasing the skids. It can make your project go more smoothly.

The following example is taken from a customer agreement my partner and I used to grease the skids for a project review we were retained to conduct. Every part of this agreement was worked out *before* a contract was signed. Having the details worked out in advance made doing the work so much easier—hence, greasing the skids. There are five parts to this example:

1. Focusing questions for the project review
2. Team deliverables for the project review
3. Roles and responsibilities for the project review
4. Logistical support on-site provided by the customer
5. Statement of work.

While many projects share some infrastructure elements, not all the details provided in the example may be directly relevant to your project. This example, however, illustrates how paying attention to the project infrastructure can be a powerful approach to project leadership. As you read over the example, you may want to begin making your own list of infrastructure elements that apply to your project.

Throughout this example, you will find text followed by comments inside a box. The boxed comments explain how the preceding text *greased the skids* for us.

Part 1: Focusing Questions for the Project Review

1. What concerns us most about the Scrumptious Serrano project right now?

There are no specific concerns. The project has completed its first phase. At this time, we consider it prudent to begin reviewing the project's plans and progress on a periodic basis going forward. By conducting periodic reviews, we hope to avoid any serious problems in the future.

> Greasing the skids: These are the customer's own words expressing any concerns about the project. This is generally why the customer is asking for a review. The answer to this question helps the review team focus its discussions and be efficient with its time while team members are interviewing project staff. The review team will address the concerns, if any, in the written review report.

2. What do we hope to learn from the review?

We hope to learn if the project's plan identified by the Blue Chile Factory is capable of achievement, or how the plan could be modified to ensure its success in the following four areas:

2.1 Executive Sponsorship

2.1.1 Have we set up executive sponsorship of the project in a manner that encourages sound decision-making and the executive attention required for success?

2.1.2 Has the project identified clearly its business objectives, including expected benefits? Will the project be able to meet these objectives and position the Blue Chile Factory to achieve the benefits?

2.1.3 The Scrumptious Serrano project appears to be headed toward a custom-built solution. We would like some verification that this is the correct approach, and that we are structured to successfully complete that project.

2.2. Business Functionality

2.2.1 Have the functional requirements been identified and approved by the future users?

2.2.2 Have the data requirements, including online accessible data and printed reports, been identified and approved by the future users?

2.2.3 Will the new system be acceptable to the various users of the system?

2.3 Management Capability

2.3.1 Is the project organized and managed in a manner that will enable us to meet the schedule, quality, and budget targets?

2.3.2 Are project risks being managed prudently?

2.4 Technical Capability and Infrastructure

2.4.1 Does the project have the resources necessary for success, including money, skilled staff, technical tools, and a development environment?

2.4.2 Is the project taking advantage of technical tools, skills, and capabilities available at the Blue Chile Factory?

2.4.3 Will our current technical infrastructure support the system during development and in production?

2.4.4 Will the new Scrumptious Serrano system be maintainable going forward?

Greasing the skids: These are the specific questions the customer wants answered. They are amazingly helpful for organizing the review and making sure that the review team members use their time most efficiently. The specificity of the particular questions takes most of the guesswork out of determining what to investigate. This particular customer needed a little coaching to achieve the desired level of specificity.

3. What can happen as a result of the review?

The review can lead us to:

3.1 Increase our confidence in the project's approach, organization, and management.

3.2 Identify and address any risks or concerns that require immediate action.

> Greasing the skids: This is what the customer hopes to get from the review. Any time you can get a customer—or boss, peer, or employee—to tell you what he hopes for, you are in a much better position to give it to him. Trying to guess this or assuming you know what he should hope for is risky. We asked ourselves periodically throughout the review process if what we were uncovering addressed these hopes.

Part 2: Team Deliverables for the Project Review

1. Verbal briefing presented by the review team.

2. Written review report delivered in person by the review team.

> Greasing the skids: This simply clarifies what the review deliverables are. Documenting this helps avoid any confusion about what will be delivered after the review is completed.

Part 3: Roles and Responsibilities for the Project Review

1. William Guerrez *(The purpose of the review is to increase your level of confidence.)*

1.1 Prior and during the review

1.1.1 Sponsors the Scrumptious Serrano project review.

1.1.2 Signs letter of engagement for consultant's services.

1.1.3 Announces the review to the Scrumptious Serrano project team members. We suggest this be done in person if possible with key project personnel and via memo for the rest, making the following key points:

1.1.3.1 That you want confidence that the plan of action for the Scrumptious Serrano project is achievable.

1.1.3.2 That you want the project team's cooperation with the review team.

1.1.3.3 That you want team members to make themselves and information about the project available to the review team.

1.1.4 Provides the review team with access to people and information. Attends mid-review verbal briefing with the review team as he chooses.

1.1.5 Receives the written review report in person.

1.1.6 Delivers the review report to the Board of Directors, supported by the review team as requested.

1.1.7 Maintains confidentiality of review information.

1.2 Post-Review

1.2.1 Makes and implements operational decisions based on the review findings and recommendations.

1.2.2 Informs the Board of operational decisions, status, and issues at regular intervals as the project progresses.

1.2.3 Maintains confidentiality of review information.

> Greasing the skids: William is the president of the Blue Chile Factory. He is the one who requested the Scrumptious Serrano project review. His support is essential to having a successful review. This part clarifies what the review team needs from him. Executives are busy people, so if you want their support, especially their time, you have to negotiate for it up front.

2. Virginia Tangoli

2.1 Finalizes letter of agreement with the consultant.

2.2 Manages the agreement during the engagement, if necessary.

2.3 Arranges for administrative support for the review team.

2.4 Prepares non-disclosure letters for review team members to sign.

2.5 Receives signed letters from review team members.

2.6 Confers with the review team on legal matters.

2.7 Receives and arranges payment for consultant's invoices.

2.8 Maintains confidentiality of review information.

> Greasing the skids: Virginia is the general counsel for the Blue Chile Factory and executive assistant to the president. Her support is also essential because she is the direct conduit to the president, and in some cases speaks for the president. She manages our contract and takes care of paying invoices.

3. Administrative/Logistical Assistance Person

We need a person available to support us who is thoroughly familiar with the company and the people being interviewed and is able to get things done quickly. We need the following kind of support from that person:

3.1 Help with arranging lodging and work areas.

3.2 Help locating staff.

3.3 Give us directions to local offices and buildings.

3.4 Schedule or reschedule interviews.

3.5 Locate and collect documents.

3.6 Arrange to copy, bind, and ship documents.

3.7 Provide supplies and materials.

Greasing the skids: A review team can spend an incredible amount of time handling all sorts of logistical and administrative tasks during a project review unless arrangements are made for the customer to provide this kind of support. This part clarifies what is expected from the administrative/logistical support person. With the administrative and logistical burdens lifted, the review team can concentrate on its primary tasks: interviewing staff, reading project documents, analyzing collected information, and writing the review report.

4. Review Team

4.1 Conduct the review as described in this agreement.

4.2 Sign nondisclosure agreements at the Blue Chile Factory's request.

4.3 Alert William Guerrez of any "red flag" issues we discover during the review as we learn about them. Caution is required before acting on red flags until the review is completed, as interim information can change.

4.4 Support William Guerrez in the manner he requests in delivery of the report to the Board of Directors.

4.5 Maintains confidentiality of review information.

Greasing the skids: This clarifies the review team's responsibilities. It helps both parties set expectations and avoid confusion about who does what. In some cases, it can be a good idea to state what the review team is *not* responsible for.

Part 4: Logistical Support On-Site Provided by the Customer

The Blue Chile Factory will provide the following:

1. Lodging

The team will need the following lodging on or near the Blue Chile Factory.

1.1 One no smoking room for April 8-17, 2002.

2. Review Team Work Center

We will be interviewing people who directly and indirectly work on the project. Our work center should be as convenient as possible to the people we will be interviewing. Typically, we will interview a person in his/her own work area because the person has easier access to project-related work products. The review team work center should:

2.1 Comfortably seat two people with desks or table work surfaces.

2.2 Be secure so that we can safely leave our laptops, documents, and personal belongings there while we are interviewing and overnight.

2.3 Have lots of wall space to post 5x8 cards or flip chart papers.

2.4 Have a flip chart easel with pad and a variety of colored markers (i.e., three each of red, black, green, blue, and orange) and masking tape.

2.5 Have a speakerphone, company phone book, and phone list of Board members.

2.6 Have a printer with cables and print driver software capable of printing high quality (laser or ink jet) output from Macintosh PowerBook computers.

3. Interview Room

We need access to a small private office with a door in the event that a person wants to be interviewed away from where he/she works. The interview room should be near the review team work center.

4. Access to Staff and Documents

Once we determine who should be interviewed and which project-related work products to review, we will need timely access to those staff and work products. We will be happy to sign a nondisclosure agreement if necessary.

> Greasing the skids: This part describes other kinds of support required, such as lodging, work area, interview room, and access to staff and documents. Not arranging for these things in advance can seriously hinder the review. You run the risk of being stuck in a too-small work area or having no work area at all. If you have no suitable work area on site, you will have to haul all your stuff with you wherever you go—such as back and forth to and from your hotel room.

Part 5: Statement of Work

Project Review—Scrumptious Serrano

Project review team—[Names of review team members] hereafter referred to as "we."

We will arrive at the Blue Chile Factory on April 7, 2002, to conduct a project review of the Scrumptious Serrano project between April 8 and April 16, 2002. We will review documents and conduct approximately 13 interviews during April 8 and 9, 2002. We will then analyze the information collected and write the review report between April 10 and April 15. We will offer a mid-review verbal briefing on Tuesday afternoon, April 9, giving the review team's general impressions of the current condition of the project, based on the interviews conducted and the documents reviewed. Upon completion of the review, we will prepare a written report and deliver it on April 16 to William Guerrez, Virginia Tangoli, Jerry Manoz, Dr. Ed Smith, Alice Ramon, and Bill Sanchones. The written report will contain the review team's observations of the current condition of the Scrumptious Serrano project. The report will also contain recommended actions. The recommended actions will be based on our understanding of the documented business objectives for the project.

The following aspects of the Scrumptious Serrano project will be reviewed:

- *Executive sponsorship*
- *Business functionality*
- *Management capability*
- *Technical capability and infrastructure.*

These aspects are stated in more detail in the section above titled "What do we hope to learn from the review?"

Review Team Schedule:

Calendar Dates (all in 2002)	Number of Consulting Days for Each Reviewer	Planned Review Work
Monday-Tuesday, April 8-9	2	Conduct interviews
Tuesday afternoon, April 9		Provide mid-review verbal briefing
Wednesday-Monday, April 10-15	4–5	Analyze collected information Develop recommendations Prepare written review report
Tuesday, April 16	1	Deliver review report

Estimated Consulting Fee and Costs:

The following range of fees and costs is our preliminary estimate for convening a two-person review team, preparing for the review, conducting the review, conducting a verbal briefing, writing the review report, and delivering the written report during the period April 8-16, 2002.

$Consulting Fee Min.—$Consulting Fee Max. equals Estimated Consulting Fee (14 days to 16 days @ [$Rate])

$Travel Expense Min.—$Travel Expense Max. equals Estimated Travel Expense

$Total Min.—$Total Max. equals Estimated Total Consulting Fee and Travel Expense

We will invoice the Blue Chile Factory for actual time spent @ [$Rate] per day per consultant and actual expenses for travel, lodging, meals, local transportation, and materials and supplies. Terms are net 30 days.

Greasing the skids: This is a summary of the work to be performed, key events, schedule, key individuals, and fees. The statement of work, along with the other five parts of the agreement, provides both the review team and the customer with enough clarity so that both parties can fine-tune the agreement. Signature blocks may be added to the agreement itself, or the agreement can become an attachment to a simple contract that references the agreement.

WAYS TO KEEP INFRASTRUCTURE IN YOUR AWARENESS

Because infrastructure is so often overlooked, it helps to have tricks or gimmicks to keep infrastructure in your awareness. One such trick is a "Hudson's Bay Start." Another gimmick is to use a checklist or a template to help you remember.

The "Hudson's Bay Start"

The first camp was merely a "pull out," commonly called for many years a "Hudson's Bay Start," very necessary so that before finally launching into the unknown one could see that nothing had been forgotten, or that if one had taken too much, being so near to the base, the mistake could be easily corrected.[1]

—Sir Samuel Benfield Steele, July 8, 1874

The term refers to the practice by Hudson Bay Company explorers, who would take their "fully provisioned" expeditions only a short distance from base headquarters and set up camp to make sure they had all the essentials for their long journey. One can think of a "Hudson's Bay Start" as a risk management tactic. A similar tactic can be applied to projects in the following ways:

- *A project to build software using a new software development environment.* First try building a small, simple piece of software (rather than building an entire complex system) from start to finish using the new environment. Use what you learn to refine your plans for building the whole system. Note infrastructure that was needed or should be added.

[1] Walter S. Avis (ed.), *A Dictionary of Canadianisms on Historical Principles* (Toronto: W.J. Gage Limited, 1967), p. 354.

- *The go-live of a system implementation project.* Stage one or more mock production implementations with replicated production data that will exercise all the production operations procedures, including backout procedures. You are probably ready for go-live when you are no longer learning anything significant from the mock implementations.
- *A trial run for an integrated system project such as Enterprise Resource Planning (ERP).* Have a real user process one type of transaction with real data—such as hire, payroll, trial balance—that touches as many modules of the ERP as possible, especially chart of accounts, from start to finish including report generation. Then verify results in all modules.
- *A new system project that forces business process changes.* Set up a "playground" environment where users can practice doing their work the new way with real (though not production) data. This will surface issues early enough to determine whether they are training issues or system issues so that they can be resolved prior to implementation.

Checklists and Templates

A checklist is a list of essential things you want to remember to do. As you do each thing, check it off the list. Here is an example of a checklist one might use when planning an ERP project to help keep infrastructure in mind:

1. Which policies, procedures, or standards will need to be modified to complete this project?
2. What new policies, procedures, or standards will need to be written and approved to complete this project?
3. Which legal contracts or regulations will need a legal review to complete this project?
4. Which human resources policies, practices, and procedures will need to be reviewed to identify impacts?
5. What impacts will this project have on existing information systems?
6. What impacts will this project have on IT development and production environments, such as developer workstations, servers, LAN, WAN, databases, and configuration management?
7. What impacts will this project have on our physical plant, such as conference rooms, work stations, copiers, voice systems, lighting, ventilation, heating and cooling?

Sometimes a checklist can become a template. A template is a reusable guide—perhaps a form—that provides the essential information categories and questions and prompts the user of the template to provide the relevant information. Here is an example of a template based on the above checklist. The project manager would be responsible for making sure that the template is completed. This particular template would require review and information from several functions such as Policies and Procedures, Legal, HR, IT, and Facilities.

Title of Project: ______________________________

Project # ______________________________

Internal Company Policies, Procedures and Standards

List any current policies, procedures and standards relevant to this project, and the nature of any changes required.

Title of Current Policy, Procedure, or Standard	Describe the changes needed to support this project:

New Policies, Procedures and Standards

Describe any *new* policies, procedures, and standards needed for this project to be successfully implemented and supported:

[New policies, procedures, and standards]

Legal Review by Corporate Counsel

☐ Please review any contracts and regulations that might impact this project or be impacted by it. Below are identified areas of potential impact.

[Potential areas of impact]

Human Resources Review by Corporate Human Resources

Please review the following areas of HR policies, practices, and procedures to identify impacts on this project or changes required to implement the project.

- ☐ Employment
- ☐ Human Resources Administration
- ☐ Training and Development

Below are identified areas of potential Human Resources impact:

[Potential areas of Human Resources impact]

Information Systems Review by Information Technology

Please review the following information application systems to identify potential impacts of this project on those systems.

Name of Information System	Nature of Potential Impact

Information Technology Environment/Architecture Review

Please address the following technology areas to identify potential impacts of this project on both the IT development and production environments. (Examples are developers' workstations, development server, LAN, WAN, databases, and configuration management.)

Name of Technology Area	**Development or Production** D=development P=production B=Both	Nature of Potential Impact

Physical Plant Review

Please address the following physical plant areas to identify and address potential impacts of this project. (Examples are conference rooms, rest rooms, work stations, copiers, voice systems, lighting, ventilation, heating and cooling, and parking.)

Name of Physical Plant Area	Nature of Potential Impact

Project Manager Signature ______________________

Date ______________________

Project Sponsor Signature ______________________

Date ______________________

To recap:

- With both cities and enterprises, infrastructure roughly means things we depend on that we do not think about much. Infrastructure seems to have the following characteristics:
  - — We need it to achieve our goals.
  - — It is part of our context, although perhaps not in the foreground of our awareness.
  - — We tend to take it for granted.
- If we apply this meaning of infrastructure much more broadly to, for instance, anything we need to achieve our individual and project goals, then we can give a name to all that stuff we need but may not think about. Naming that stuff means we can plan for it.
- Infrastructure can apply to a single task or a multitask project.
- Providing the right infrastructure for your project is like greasing the skids. It can make your project go much more smoothly.
- Infrastructure is so often overlooked that it helps to have tricks or gimmicks to keep infrastructure in our awareness. One such trick is called a "Hudson's Bay Start." Another is the use of a checklist or template.

Try this:

1. Recall a recent project, either personal or professional. Were there any infrastructure items that you eventually discovered you needed but did not plan for at the beginning of the project? If so, what were they? How could you have tricked yourself into thinking of those items sooner?
2. If you are currently involved in a project, which parts of its infrastructure, if any, might you be overlooking right now?

Chapter 17
WHEN YOU KNOW SOMETHING IS WRONG

You may know when a project is in trouble long before the project is openly declared a failure or out of control. I hesitate to use the word "openly." In my experience, one of the largest contributors to failed projects is that people cannot talk openly about their project's problems. Talking openly about project problems is precisely what is needed to help avoid failure.

One of the ways you can know in advance that a project is in trouble is by how you feel. The feelings may come gradually from the accumulation of many different observations, each of which alone might seem trivial but collectively they are significant. The feelings may come from a single observation that triggers a painful memory from a past project.

With many projects, there is no structure that allows such feelings to be openly expressed. So the feelings may remain unexpressed or may come out as nervous humor or whispered comments. You may perceive that too much is at stake to make a fuss about your feelings: career, money, ego, and business success, to name a few. Often there is so much momentum that it is difficult for you to know what to do with your feelings. It is easier to trust that things will work themselves out eventually. It is easier to put your head down and keep working.

Some examples of feelings that might go with troubled projects:
Afraid, anxious, ashamed, clueless, crazy, determined, helpless, hopeless, incompetent, lost, mad, nervous, numb, scared, sick, worried.

Some very experienced project leaders develop a kind of wisdom about this. Over many projects, they learn to associate some feelings with specific behaviors that almost always lead to serious trouble.

One example of a specific behavior is that the project sponsor is too busy. He or she is not accessible to hear about critical problems, clear roadblocks, or make sponsor-designated decisions. A wise project leader will recognize this behavior immediately as very serious. A less wise project leader may have a nagging feeling about it, but will not appreciate how serious this behavior is. If allowed to continue, this behavior will put the project at serious risk. This is why it is so important that a project leader's domain knowledge and project scale experience be appropriately matched to the project.

For example, you may have lots of experience leading small teams of four or five people. That does not mean that you are appropriately matched for a project team of 100 people. You may have lots of functional experience with financials or payroll. That does not mean that you can lead an ERP implementation.

When you are inappropriately matched to your project, you can inadvertently treat some observations as trivial because you do not understand the possible effects. I have witnessed the appointment of a project director on a multimillion dollar project who had no experience whatsoever managing an IT project. This person was intelligent and motivated, but simply did not understand the significance of project events or nonevents that could dramatically affect his project.

The problems in your project may be reflected in your body. Whether or not you consciously connect your feelings to what is happening with your project, your body has a way of letting you know something is wrong. Some people get headaches. Some get stomachaches. Others may notice an increase in neck and back problems. Other physiological symptoms can include a tight chest, frequent sighing, clenched fists, digestive tract irritations, or unexplained rashes.

Troubled projects do not necessarily cause these symptoms. I am suggesting that if you have these or other symptoms, your body is telling you that something is wrong. The choice is yours to decide what to do with that information.

A group of experienced IT professionals got together at a 2000 Leaders' Forum[1] session to share their considerable project wisdom. The group talked about specific behaviors they had learned to associate with worried feelings on projects. I participated in the discussion. The following table is my rendering of some of the ideas discussed in that session.

---

[1]A week-long event hosted by Strider & Cline, Inc., held annually. Contributors to the session were Paul Castellano, Esther Derby, Bruce Eckel, Dale Emery, Frank Huebner, Pat Medvick, Robert Snipp, Eileen Strider, Wayne Strider, and Marty Vik. Esther Derby facilitated the session.

How do I know my project is in trouble?
Leaders' Forum, 6/29/00, Mount Crested Butte, CO

Do Not Pass Go	Follow the Yellow Brick Road	No Adult Supervision	Night of the Living Dead	Schedule Fantasies	The Great and Powerful Oz	Are We There Yet?
• No business owner evident • No customer involvement evident • Distracted by technology	• Project documents not updated • No process for scope changes • Require-ments keep changing	• Issue logs not being worked • Decision-making at the wrong level • Closed human communica-tion • Denial instead of solutions • Progress stated in abstract terms	• People unhappy and distracted • Increased attrition rate • Increasing number of people getting sick • Overtime the standard • Resources overcommit-ted and unfocused	• Schedule apparently more important than quality • Intention to make up the schedule slippage later • Expected delivery dates vary	• Arrival of outside consultant • Pep talks • Reorganizing again?	• No "go-live" criteria • Definition of "done" • No deliverables

I have seen these behaviors throughout my career and had feelings about them. I did not always make a conscious connection between my feelings and the behaviors I was seeing, especially early in my career. After lots of experience, I now know what to look for when I start having certain feelings. I also know that when I find these behaviors, I will soon get a familiar feeling. It works both ways for me.

DO NOT PASS GO

These behaviors are serious enough to stop the project until they are corrected.

No Business Owner Evident

Your project needs someone to accept the role and responsibility of business owner. The owner is usually the person who requested the project, believing that it will provide an economic benefit for his or her organization. The owner is also the one who directly or indirectly approves the commitment of resources toward the project and is accountable for the resulting business effects. The owner is the one who ultimately evaluates the goodness of the project.

If you cannot identify a business owner for your project, proceed no further until you do. Do not be satisfied with an unofficial verbal acknowledgment by the business owner. Insist on getting the role fully described in writing, along with the business owner's signature.

No Customer Involvement Evident

Your project needs at least one customer to be viable; however, it may have multiple customers. Very often customers figure heavily in determining your project's success or failure. If none of your project's customers is involved in any way that you can discern, be alarmed.

One example of this might be technical staff writing functional requirements with little or no user input or feedback. Give this issue the highest visibility possible. Make sure that the business owner and executive sponsor understand that this is a serious risk to the project's success. Insist on customer involvement before proceeding. Negotiate with each customer its level of involvement and specific responsibilities. Document both in writing and get signatures.

Distracted by Technology

Technology projects need to be driven by business objectives. Initiating a project for no other reason than having the latest technology could be considered fiscally irresponsible. There is nothing wrong with wanting the latest technology. Having it may indeed provide some economic benefits. It is critical that a business need/benefits discussion take place. Do not leave it to chance that there might be economic benefits.

Ask a question like, "How does this project support your business strategy?" or "What business problem does this project solve?" Listen carefully for answers that you recognize are relevant to the business. An example might be, "We need this technology to maintain our competitive position. It solves a sticky security problem that is causing us to lose customers."

FOLLOW THE YELLOW BRICK ROAD

These behaviors can prevent you from knowing the real condition of your project and lead to your project getting out of control before you realize it.

Project Documents Not Updated

When project documents are not kept current, it is very difficult to understand the current truth of your project. Project documents can include work plans, staffing plans, estimates, Gantt charts, hill climbing charts, issue logs, progress reports, budgets, test plans, work breakdown structures, scope change requests. Any project documents that your organization uses to manage project information should be kept up to date. Without current, accurate information, you cannot know the truth about your project or what corrective action, if any, needs to be taken—and your project is at serious risk.

No Process for Scope Changes

The inability to control project scope—scope creep—has sunk many projects. A written and approved scope change request process can help enormously in controlling scope creep. Such a process takes the burden off you, the lonely project leader, of saying yes or no to scope changes. Properly done, the process can openly inform the appropriate decision-makers of the impacts of the scope change on cost, schedule, and quality. This does not guarantee that the scope will not change, but it can encourage healthy discussion and more informed decisions.

Requirements Keep Changing

Users and owners evaluate goodness based on how well their requirements have been met. It is important to remember that a requirements document is *not* the requirements—it is merely a representation of the requirements discovered at a point in time. Requirements are in the minds of the users and owners. The requirements document is someone's best effort, however imperfect, to get the requirements out of the users' minds and down on paper.

There is nothing wrong with changing requirements as long as there is a process for evaluating and approving the impact of the changes on project schedule, cost, and quality. With no such process in place, almost anyone can change the requirements without understanding the effects on the project. When that happens, you will ultimately have to deal with the resulting resource issues and you could look like the incompetent one when the schedule slips or the cost goes up.

NO ADULT SUPERVISION

These behaviors can make it difficult for you to manage day-to-day problems and opportunities effectively. Important project work can fall through the cracks if these behaviors are allowed to persist.

Issue Logs Not Being Worked

High priority issues reported as *open* on issue logs week after week should always show up on your worry radar. Your *worry radar* lets you know when something important needs your attention. For some it is an intuition. Others keep a worry list on their whiteboard. A worry list can simply be a list of behaviors that cause you to take action immediately.

There can be many reasons why an issue remains open week after week, but it is wise to investigate as soon as you notice. Some of the reasons could include:

- The issue has not been assigned to anyone.
- The issue has been assigned, but the responsible person does not have the skill, experience, or resources to resolve it.
- The responsible person is overloaded with higher priority work.

Whatever the reasons, if issue logs are not being worked, it points to a general lack of management attention. This leads one to question what else is not getting management attention.

Decision-making at the Wrong Level

The symptoms of this behavior can include:

- Decisions are not made at all.
- Decisions are made, and then later reversed or ignored.
- Decisions are made, followed by lots of grumbling and second-guessing.
- Decisions are eventually made, but the context has changed, rendering the decisions inappropriate.

The right level for decision-making is the lowest possible level. The lowest possible level is the level at which the decision-maker has the necessary information, contextual perspective, and organizational authority and responsibility to act. When decisions are pushed to a management level higher than necessary, people may be puzzled or disappointed with the result: a decision they do not like or no decision at all. When decisions are pushed too low, sometimes the decision-maker languishes and never actually decides anything, or makes a decision that no one supports.

Closed Human Communication

Communication is said to be "closed" when information can come in but not go out. In other words, information is available, but some people on the project have the information they need and others do not. Some people are working with current information and others are using outdated information. Rumors seem to be a primary information source.

Certain techniques help open up communication: consistent format for all status reports and issue logs, a communications clearinghouse manager who is responsible for making sure that project information is consistent, accurate, current, and distributed quickly to the people who need it, and regular all-hands meetings during which accurate information is shared and current rumors are solicited and clarified.

Denial Instead of Solutions

Sometimes denial becomes the apparent solution method of choice. The most serious evidence of this is when you hear nothing at all about problems that you know exist. Still serious but less so are comments such as "It's not that serious," "No problem here," "They did it to us," "We can make that up, no sweat," "It will get better when. . . ." These kind of comments imply that something is wrong, yet deny the impact or project it onto someone else.

A powerful project leader will not tolerate denial. Summoning his courage during a project management meeting, he might say something like, "I am not going to proceed until we talk about why we cannot talk about what is wrong with our project."

Progress Stated in Abstract Terms

Progress reports stated in terms of activity instead of progress worry me. When I read a progress report that says things like, "I worked on the eight ball module," "I attended a meeting," or "I talked to Mr. Taylor," I want to say, "So what?" "What did you complete?" "What remains to be completed?" "When will the eight ball module be completed?" "Is there anything that can be completed ahead of schedule?"

Let's say that a work package has 20 tasks to be completed in 12 weeks. Ten tasks are completed in 8 weeks. Fifty percent complete, right? A status report says, "We should be able to catch up in the next 4 weeks." With only 4 weeks left, 10 tasks are due, yet the actual experience is that 10 tasks took 8 weeks. Why would anyone think the work package can be finished in time? Are the remaining 10 tasks that much easier? What if they are harder? Will people work overtime? Perhaps resources will be added? Exactly how will productivity be increased by 200 percent? The answer is what I would like to read in the status report.

NIGHT OF THE LIVING DEAD

When you notice these behaviors, burnout is imminent. If these behaviors are allowed to persist, project productivity will continue to decrease at an increasing rate until the project collapses from exhaustion.

People Unhappy and Distracted

You may notice people being short with each other or outright hostile. You may see people making more than their normal number of mental errors. People have various ways of coping with the stress of a troubled project: some shut down, some check out, some walk around like zombies, some hide, some get sick, some medicate themselves with alcohol, drugs, or sex, and some give up and quit.

Increased Attrition Rate

You notice that people are leaving (or trying to leave) your project in increasing numbers, at more than your typical attrition rate. Exit interviews may or may not reveal any links to project health. It is a good idea to review exit interview data regardless.

Increasing Number of People Getting Sick

More people are getting sick, ranging from minor to serious physical and emotional illness. And people are staying sick longer. Productivity drops. The remaining people pick up the slack for a while, then they also begin getting sick.

Overtime the Standard

When overtime becomes the status quo instead of a periodic recovery technique, you can expect unhappy and distracted staff, an increased attrition rate, and illness to follow.

Resources Overcommitted and Unfocused

You may notice that the same individuals are assigned to multiple work packages. If you add up each individual's percentage time on all the packages, you might find that he or she is overcommitted. I have seen this on project staffing plans: Tom is assigned to work package alpha @ 50 percent, work package bravo @ 50 percent, work package charlie @ 50 percent, and work package delta @ 50 percent, all during the same calendar time period without overtime. Using 35 hours per week to estimate one full-time equivalent (FTE), that would mean that Tom is committed to 70 hours per week. This is what I would call overcommitted. If Tom were expected to work overtime as well, he could be on a fast path to burnout.

By "unfocused," I mean splitting time on too many tasks. When my time is split among several tasks (e.g., 20 percent on project x task, 50 percent on project y task, 30 percent on project z task), some time and focus will be lost as I switch between those tasks. (For more on this see the table in Chapter 15, Substitutes for Time.)

SCHEDULE FANTASIES

These behaviors can lead to false hopes for customers, unrealistic expectations for management, and disappointment all around.

Schedule Apparently More Important Than Quality

Sometimes schedule really is more important than quality. When all users, owners, and sponsors are in explicit agreement about this, I do not get too worried. I do get worried, however, when I hear them say that quality is more important than schedule but they behave as if schedule is more important than quality. A common example of this is when a project starts to slip seriously and the time is recovered by cutting back on testing.

It is a fact of project life that schedule, quality, and cost are continually being traded off. Scope changes, requirements changes, funding changes—these events all trigger discussions about the effects on schedule, quality, and cost on healthy projects that have open processes for handling these kinds of changes. In the absence of such processes, it can be very stressful when you get mixed messages about which is more important. If key decision-makers resist your best attempts to clarify this, you would be wise to document carefully any decisions relating to your project's schedule, quality, and cost.

Intention to Make Up the Schedule Slippage Later

This sounds good; occasionally, it works out that way. But it usually does not. When reviewing projects that are slipping schedule, I like to look at the actual experience data. Knowing that there are no perfect estimates, I have an open mind about the possibility of making up slippage. However, I want to be convinced. I want to know:

- Which tasks can be pulled in (completed earlier than scheduled)?
- What will cause your team's productivity to increase dramatically over its historical productivity?

Suppose your team estimates that it can complete 10 work packages per week, 160 in four months (graphically displayed in the chart on the following page). They start in January. Historical performance during January and February has been 5 work packages per week. To finish 160 work packages by April, your team will have to be three times as productive as they have been. What is going to cause that to happen?

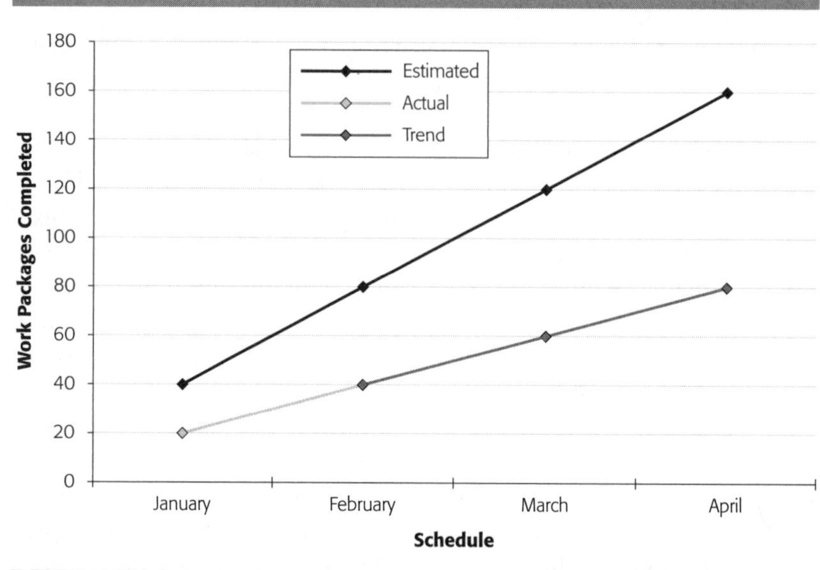

Expected Delivery Dates Vary

Management sometimes alters the expected delivery date depending on the audience. The customer might hear one date and the project team might hear another. That is not unusual. But when multiple conflicting delivery dates become the norm, one has to wonder, What is the definition of "delivery"? Does management trust us? Do they trust each other? Do I trust them? At the beginning of the project, these questions might not seem significant. But when the pressure is on and every minute counts, the people doing the work want to know how much time they have and what the real expected delivery date is.

Lack of clarity around delivery dates can be perceived as management playing games. This perception can adversely affect project team morale.

THE GREAT AND POWERFUL OZ

When you see these behaviors, consider them confirmation that your project is in serious trouble. Take a peek behind the curtain to see who is really there before you decide what to do next.

Arrival of Outside Consultant

You may hear an announcement that a consultant from Project Masters of the Universe, Inc. (PMU), will be visiting your project. The consultant will poke around for a few days and give an objective report to management on the status of your project. This confirms your worst suspicions. Something must really be wrong if management is bringing in a PMU consultant. You might be relieved if it were not for your knowledge that PMU has hoards of programmers waiting in the wings to take over your project. You will not be surprised if the consultant recommends outsourcing project completion to PMU.

It can be useful and healthy for a project to have an independent, objective review. However, the review should be conducted by a firm that does not sell solutions to the problems found and that is not affiliated with any vendors. You will be more likely to get an objective review from such a consultant.

Pep Talks

"Management is really counting on you!" "We know you won't let us down." "There is a lot at stake with this project." These are some of the exhortations I have heard from executives at all-hands meetings. I usually hear these kinds of comments only when there is some concern about the project—almost never when things are going well. Come to think of it, I rarely see an executive unless something is wrong. The combination—an executive, at an all-hands meeting, giving a pep talk—is overwhelming evidence of serious trouble.

Reorganizing Again?

Sometimes reorganizing is a good thing to do when there is a specific reason or problem to solve. For example, a specific reason might be to realign the project to respond to changes in the market, satisfy venture capitalists, or merge with another company to take advantage of specific expertise. But continually reorganizing the project structure for no apparent reason can be disruptive. In an organization where communication is open, one could reasonably ask, "What is the problem to be solved by reorganizing?" Another good question is "What does it cost us to reorganize?"

These two questions can open a healthy dialogue. Where communication is closed, these questions probably would not be asked in the first place. If they were asked, they probably would not be answered in any way that would make sense to you.

Sometimes, regardless of whether communication is open or closed, reorganizing is the only problem-solving tool in the management tool kit. In these organizations, reorganizing is always the solution—no matter what the problem is.

ARE WE THERE YET?

Some projects seem to go on and on forever. Some finish before they should—meaning that they "go-live" before they are ready. Often projects go on and on because there is no clear definition of "done." The following behaviors make it nearly impossible to know when your project is ready to go-live or when it is done.

No "Go-Live" Criteria

Your project team has worked hard for 14 months on the Sweet Habanero development. They have coded and tested. They have trained the users. They have practiced backout procedures. Go-live is imminent. How does your team know they are ready for go-live? How good is good enough? For some project teams, the only criterion for go-live is that the schedule says we go-live on this date—whether we are ready or not—as if there were no choice. Wiser project teams know they have a choice and feel responsible for choosing wisely.

One way of choosing wisely is to have some prenegotiated criteria in the form of a checklist. Prior to go-live, key decision-makers from project management, user management, business owners, and executive sponsors meet to go over each criterion one by one, agree on its current status, and, after having reviewed all criteria jointly, agree to go or no-go. A no-go decision has no stigma attached to it because it is arrived at by the joint wisdom of all the key parties. This group knows that going live when not ready can be very risky. Typically, the no-go decision will be accompanied by a list of corrective actions that must be accomplished before a go decision can be made.

My partner Eileen Strider adds that setting a next go-live opportunity date can be a wise thing to do. The go-live decision will be revisited on that date to make sure that the corrective actions are completed.

Definition of "Done"

When is a project done? Some projects seem to linger on and never end. Here are a few possible signals that a project is done:

- When all the people are transferred to other projects
- When go-live is successful
- Thirty days after go-live, when post-implementation support has transitioned to ongoing support
- When the project post mortem or retrospective is completed
- When the project closeout presentation is made to management
- When the development software is turned over to the maintenance team
- When the user has certified the system
- When you start on the next release.

A good time to define "done" is at the beginning of your project. That way, your project team can recognize when it is done. The team can effect an orderly shutdown. Without such a definition, your project could be at risk of never ending. If it does end, the shutdown could be very jolting.

No Deliverables

A good project plan will identify deliverables—physical artifacts—in addition to activities. A deliverable can be a requirements document, a source code listing, a test plan, or a report. A deliverable can be anything that you can see and touch. It is the evidence that someone's work produced something. Checking deliverables is a good way to measure project progress. Progress means getting work done and having something to show for it. No deliverables means no progress.

This is why I have a problem with activity-based status reports. It is too hard to tell if anything is getting done. I can see that people are working, but without deliverables I have no reliable way of knowing if progress is being made.

LEGITIMIZE FEELINGS IN YOUR PROJECT TEAM

A powerful project leader will want as much information about his or her project as possible. Feelings are information too. Legitimize feelings in your project team. One way to do this is to solicit feeling information in project meetings along with other kinds of information. You can do this by asking an open question like, "Does anybody have any excitements or concerns to express? If your team members are not used to expressing feeling information, it may take some time for them to warm up to the idea. You can help this along by expressing your own excitements and concerns. Appreciate those who express their feelings. Having a safe forum for expressing feelings can free up creative energy for problem-solving.

You may want to follow up on some of the feelings, especially concerns. They might enable you to identify and resolve a problem before it gets any worse. The worst thing you can do is try to tell someone why he should not feel how he feels or ridicule him.

CONDUCT PROJECT REVIEWS

Sometimes even a powerful project leader has difficulty convincing management that a project is in trouble. The telltale behaviors and the feelings of project members may not be enough. That's when you need an outside expert to conduct a project review and provide a written report of findings and recommendations.

An outside expert is someone with enough credentials that your management will believe him or her. A consultant may validate your fears and perhaps find more to worry about. He or she may tell management exactly the same thing you did. Go figure. Sometimes this is what it takes.

Most consultants have a template and a process for conducting project reviews. A good consultant will ask you what you are worried about. The behaviors that may trigger feelings discussed in this chapter are some of the things I look for when I review projects. These could form a starter template for you to use with your consultant.

To recap:

1. People often know when a project is in trouble long before the project is openly declared a failure or out of control.
2. One of the ways people know in advance about trouble is by how they feel.
3. Very experienced project leaders eventually learn, over many projects, to associate their feelings with specific behaviors that almost always lead to serious trouble.
4. You may feel it in your body when something is wrong with your project. We each feel this in our own unique ways.
5. Certain behaviors during projects almost always lead to trouble.
6. Legitimize and encourage the expression of feelings in your project team. Feelings are information you cannot afford to ignore.
7. A project review by an outside expert can help you convince your management that your project is trouble.

Try this:

1. Find a small group of colleagues who have participated in lots of projects. Arrange a brown bag lunch discussion using a topic like, "How do I know my project is in trouble?" or "Where do I feel it in my body when my project is in trouble?" Compare your lunch group's answers to the list of specific behaviors in this chapter.
2. In a future project team meeting, try asking a question like, "What concerns you most about our project right now?" Add that you would like to hear from each person. It is not necessary to try to fix each person's concern. The important thing is that each person have the opportunity to express it. Later, record in your journal what it was like for you to ask the question and what it was like for you to hear the answers.

POSTSCRIPT

After I finished writing this book, some of the reviewers asked if I would provide some advice on implementing my suggestions for developing powerful project leadership skills. I am better at showing people their own wisdom than at giving advice. Rather than give advice, I will try to honor their request by interpreting the following quote as it relates to implementing my suggestions:

"We only learn from those whom we love."

—Goethe

I do not pretend to know what the author meant by this, but here is how it relates to implementing my suggestions for developing powerful project leadership skills. The place to begin is always with yourself—the self part of self, other, and context. That is why Part One is about leading yourself. Learn from yourself about yourself. Others can help you learn about yourself, but you must take responsibility for your own learning. To do that well, you will need to love yourself. You know, the kind of love that is curious, patient, persistent, and forgiving.

Developing your powerful project leadership skills as I have suggested by way of stories, examples, and exercises is a long-term process, not an event. I think of it as a life-long process—sometimes smooth and sometimes bumpy—and you are never really "done."

Appendix A
WORKSHOPS

Here are some workshops that will provide opportunities to develop your self-awareness and people skills.

A few of the workshops have prerequisites for participation, so be sure to check with the workshop provider before enrolling. All these workshops are experiential by design. If you are unfamiliar with experiential learning, be sure to discuss your learning objectives and preferences with the workshop provider and understand "how it works." I have personally attended all these workshops, some more than once. These workshops have supported my personal and professional growth.

Workshop	**Contact Information**
Powerful Project Leadership	Strider & Cline, Inc. 7420 N. Granby Ave. Kansas City, MO 64151 (816) 746-8100 info@striderandcline.com www.striderandcline.com
Leaders' Forum *Attendance by invitation only. Contact Strider & Cline to find out how to receive an invitation.*	Strider & Cline, Inc. 7420 N. Granby Ave. Kansas City, MO 64151 (816) 746-8100 info@striderandcline.com www.striderandcline.com

Workshop	Contact Information
Congruent Leadership Change Shop (The Change Shop)	Weinberg & Weinberg 10131 Coors Rd. NW, I-2 Suite 303 Albuquerque, NM 87114 (505) 897-9707 hardpretzel@earthlink.net www.geraldmweinberg.com
System Effectiveness Management (SEM)	Weinberg & Weinberg 10131 Coors Rd. NW, I-2 Suite 303 Albuquerque, NM 87114 (505) 897-9707 hardpretzel@earthlink.net www.geraldmweinberg.com
Masterful Facilitation	Yarbrough Group 1113 Spruce Street Boulder, Colorado 80302 (303) 449-7107 information@yarbroughgroup.com www.yarbroughgroup.com
Performance Development Program (The Satir Year-Long)	Satir Systems 87 S. Elliott Road, Suite 212 Chapel Hill, NC 27514 (877) 967-2520 info@satirsystems.com www.satirsystems.com
Congruent Leadership Development Workshop (LDW)	Satir Systems 87 S. Elliott Road, Suite 212 Chapel Hill, NC 27514 (877) 967-2520 info@satirsystems.com www.satirsystems.com

Workshop	Contact Information
Personal Development Workshop (PDW)	Satir Systems 87 S. Elliott Road, Suite 212 Chapel Hill, NC 27514 (877) 967-2520 info@satirsystems.com www.satirsystems.com
Mastering Projects Workshop	True North, pgs, Inc. P. O. Box 1532, Walla Walla, WA 99362 (509) 527-9773 tn@ix.netcom.com www.projectcommunity.com
Power & Leadership Conference (The Power Lab)	Power & Systems, Inc. P.O. Box 990288 Prudential Station Boston, MA 02199-0288 (800) 241-0598 info@powerandsystems.com www.powerandsystems.com

Appendix B
BIBLIOGRAPHY

Many of these books deal with self-awareness and how to get better at working with people. Some are specific to technical work such as software development. Others are broader in scope. A few are just plain insightful, offering unusual or thought-provoking material related to understanding human beings. For example, *The Tipping Point* contains many examples that illustrate the power of context. I have all these books in my professional library.

Andreas, Connirae, and Tamara Andreas. *Core Transformation: Reaching the Wellspring Within* (Moab, UT: Real People Press, 1994).

Bechtold, Richard D. *Essentials of Software Project Management* (Vienna, VA: Management Concepts, 1999).

Brooks, Frederick P., Jr. *The Mythical Man-Month: Essays on Software Engineering* (Reading, MA: Addison-Wesley Publishing Company, 1995).

Chapman, Gary, and Betty Hassler. *Communication and Intimacy* (Nashville: LifeWay Press, 1992).

Crum, Thomas F. *The Magic of Conflict: Turning a Life of Work into a Work of Art* (New York: Simon & Schuster, 1987).

Dorner, Dietrich. *The Logic of Failure: Why Things Go Wrong and What We Can Do to Make Them Right* (New York: Metropolitan Books, Henry Holt and Company, 1989).

Gause, Donald C., and Gerald M. Weinberg. *Are Your Lights On? How to Figure Out What the Problem Really Is* (New York: Dorset House Publishing, 1990).

Gibb, Jack R. *Trust: A New View of Personal and Organizational Development* (Los Angeles: Guild of Tutors Press, 1978).

Gladwell, Malcolm. *The Tipping Point: How Little Things Can Make a Big Difference* (Boston: Little, Brown and Company, 2000).

Glassman, Bernard. *Bearing Witness: A Zen Master's Lessons in Making Peace* (New York: Bell Tower, 1998).

Goleman, Daniel. *Working with Emotional Intelligence* (New York: Bantam Books, 1998).

Karten, Naomi. *Managing Expectations: Working with People Who Want More, Better, Faster, NOW!* (New York: Dorset House Publishing, 1994).

Keirsey, David, and Marilyn Bates. *Please Understand Me: Character and Temperament Types* (Del Mar, CA: Prometheus Nemesis Book Company, 1984).

Oshry, Barry. *Seeing Systems: Unlocking the Mysteries of Organizational Life* (San Franscisco: Berrett-Kochler Publishers, Inc., 1995).

Page-Jones, Meiler. *Practical Project Management* (New York: Dorset House Publishing, 1985).

Palmer, Parker J. *Let Your Life Speak: Listening for the Voice of Vocation* (San Francisco: Jossey-Bass, 2000).

Satir, Virginia. *Making Contact* (Berkeley: Celestial Arts, 1976).

Satir, Virginia. *The New Peoplemaking* (Mountain View, CA: Science and Behavior Books, Inc., 1988).

Satir, Virginia, John Banmen, Jane Gerber, and Maria Gomori. *The Satir Model: Family Therapy and Beyond* (Palo Alto, CA: Science and Behavior Books, Inc., 1991).

Schaef, Anne Wilson, and Diane Fassel. *The Addictive Organization* (San Francisco: Harper and Row, 1988).

Seashore, Charles N., Edith W. Seashore, and Gerald M. Weinberg. *What Did You Say? The Art of Giving and Receiving Feedback* (Columbia, MD: Bingham House Books, 1997).

Weinberg, Gerald M. *Becoming a Technical Leader: An Organic Problem-Solving Approach* (New York: Dorset House Publishing, 1986).

Weinberg, Gerald M. *Quality Software Management Series* (New York: Dorset House Publishing), Vol. 1: *Systems Thinking* (1992). Vol. 2: *First-Order Measurement* (1993); Vol. 3: *Congruent Action* (1994), Vol. 4: Anticipating Change (1997).

INDEX

D

E

F

K

L

M

N

O

P

R

S

T

U

V

W

Y

Z